THE WEAPONLESS WARRIORS

by
Richard Kim

©Ohara Publications, Incorporated 1974
All rights reserved
Printed in the United States of America
Library of Congress Catalog Card Number: 74-21218

Ninth Printing 1982
ISBN No. 0-89750-041-5

EDITED BY JOHN SCURA

OHARA PUBLICATIONS, INCORPORATED
BURBANK, CALIFORNIA

DEDICATION
To my wife, who stood by me always.

ACKNOWLEDGEMENT

I am indebted to countless people for their help in researching and writing this book. To thank all of them individually here would be next to impossible. However, my sincerest thanks must be given to my sensei, Yoshida Kotaro, my students James Miyagi of Hawaii, Richard Lee of France, Peter Urban of New York (at whose insistence I finally undertook the writing of this book), and the following California students: Robert Leong, Cal Avila, A. Molinar, Ernie Wong, Selby Haussermann and Mr. and Mrs. Charles Siani. I would also like to express my thanks to the staff of KARATE ILLUSTRATED and BLACK BELT Magazines, without whose help I would not have known where to begin. And finally, I express my appreciation to my brother, Dr. Robert Kim, whose advice and suggestion made this manuscript a reality.

Richard Kim
San Francisco, California
1974

ABOUT THE AUTHOR

Richard Kim may well be the most knowledgeable man alive in the martial arts field. He has earned this distinction after years of work and study with scores of recognized masters throughout the world. As early as 1926, he mastered the rudiments of judo from Kaneko-sensei. At about the same time, he was gaining a foundation in karate from Arakaki, Yabu Kentsu's disciple.

In 1933, Kim found himself in Honolulu, furthering his knowledge of karate under the direction of Tachibana. Two years later, he had graduated from high school and was Orient-bound to further his study in the field. This came only after two years at the University of Hawaii, which failed to satisfy his taste.

In Shanghai, a Taoist priest named Chao Hsu Lai trained Richard Kim in the art of Shorinjiryu Kenpo and through this and his association with a direct disciple of Kotaro Yoshida, he gained entrance into the Butokukai in Japan.

After the war, Kim continued to shuttle back and forth between the U.S. and Japan in the interest of learning more about the martial arts. It was not until 1959 that he made a permanent residence of San Francisco, California.

But during the interim, he studied with such notables as Gogen Yamaguchi, and impressed Hirose Kinjo as being a walking karate encyclopedia.

Since his move to San Francisco, Richard Kim has continued his travels and his learning. He presently writes a monthly column for *Karate Illustrated* Magazine as well as spreading his knowledge to his many San Francisco students, for which he was given the 1973 karate Sensei of the Year Award in the Black Belt Hall of Fame.

Gichin Funakoshi delivers a speech to constituents at a martial arts forum (right). Below, Choki Motobu demonstrates a reverse elbow strike to one of his students, one of the many techniques which contributed to his renown.

A meeting of great karate practitioners took place in the Spring of 1948 as Mabuni Kenwa greeted Gichin Funakoshi at the Osaka railway station (right center). Standing in the background (left to right) are Sakagami Ryusho, Obata Isao and M. Nakayama, Chief Instructor of Nippon Karate Kyokai. At right, Funakoshi poses with his students shortly before an exhibition for Prince Hirohito on March 6, 1921.

To the left, a rare photograph of instructors from the Okinawan Karate-Do as they gathered in Okinawa in October, 1936. Seated left to right are Kyan Chotoku, Yabu Kentsu, Hanashiro Chomo and Miyagi Chojun. Standing are Shiroma Shimpan (far left) and Chibana Chosin (second from right).

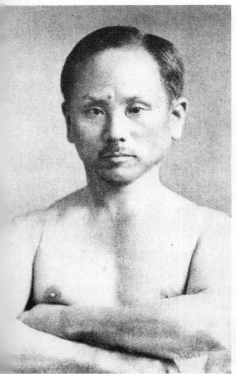

Above left, the great Funakoshi poses at age 53. To the right, the author stands alongside the late Yoshida Kotaro in Japan, circa 1945.

PREFACE

The text of this book represents my own approach to the illustrious history of karate. Like so many of the formal history studies that we have had to plod through at one time or another during our lives, this book is not intended to be an encyclopedic and linear presentation. That would require more patience and documentation than I, or any other previous karate historian, have at hand.

This instead, will be an endeavor which views the course of Okinawan karate through its most significant practitioners. These men, sensei and scoundrels alike, were folk heroes of their times and have crossed over into the realm of legend through both the written and verbal tradition of their followers. In order to keep a certain degree of continuity, I have elected to present them in a more or less chronological order.

In studying the history of karate, one is frustrated every inch of the way by conflicting testimony and a general sparsity of information. In fact, you might even call it a task of Sisyphean proportions, for separating the wheat from the chaff is like rolling a boulder to the top of a hill only to have it roll down again of its own weight.

Each of the conflicting statements probably has some validity, and it therefore becomes impossible to erect a skeletal system that is supported by dates and events as most histories are presented. Instead, our best remaining alternative would be to approach the history of karate through the colorful personalities who have contributed to the development of the art and its traditions.

I believe this book is the first to deal exclusively with the lives of the Okinawan greats. Through the stories depicting the lives of these Okinawan masters, we are better equipped to see how that particular society molded the type of martial art which we study with such fascination today.

Although the main part of this book devotes itself to studying Okinawan karate practitioners as "weaponless warriors," numerous allusions will be made to the traditional weaponry of their times. In these photos, Richard Kim illustrates the usage of these weapons: the *nunchaku* (top left), the *sai* (top right), and the *tonfa* as applied to a *bo* attack (bottom).

CONTENTS

Yara

IT WAS A CHILLY NOVEMBER DAY on the very eve of the Eighteenth century. On the other side of the globe, the Francis Bacons and Rene Descarteses were inching toward their destiny, on the verge of unleashing what we have since come to call "the Age of Enlightenment." England had a Parliamentary government and the rest of Europe was consumed in colonial greed.

But the young man who stood atop the hill overlooking the Foochow harbor at Fukien, China, was conscious only of the brisk sea breeze which incessantly blew against his face and rung in his ears. He thoughtfully stared at the horizon, comatose, in the direction of the Ryukyu Islands.

"You are homesick," declared the old man who had been standing beside him, observing his state. "Do not worry, my student," he continued, "for soon you shall be home."

The young man turned and looked at his elder. It was now 20 years since he left his village in Okinawa and had come to China to learn the martial arts from this old man.

"I am wondering whether things are the same back home in my village," said Yara, the young man.

"All phenomena is impermanent, according to Buddha. The old are gone and the young have grown old," instructed the old man.

THE WEAPONLESS WARRIORS

Yara had come from the village of Chatan[1] on the main island in the Ryukyus. He had been away from his home since he was twelve years old.

As a boy, Yara found his first years away from home difficult. He had to learn a new language as well as proficiency in the martial arts. The latter was probably the most difficult task since the discipline of learning was foreign to him. In Okinawa, he was always in touch with the wind, the sea and the typhoons that roared up from the South China Seas. Nature was his only teacher, and the only school he had ever attended was the outdoors. Yet, one day 20 years before, his uncle had come down from Naha to take him away.

His uncle, a trader, had convinced Yara's parents after a long talk that their little son, who was strong as a bull, would make a great martial artist. They agreed with him that China was the place to learn.[2]

Thus began Yara's time as deshi (apprentice) of Wong Chung-Yoh, during which he received the spiritual discipline his brute force so badly required. Under Wong's tutelage, he became a martial artist.

During his stay in China, Yara spent most of his physical energies on the art of the bo and the twin swords. He devoted himself feverishly to these weapons, day after day and year after year, until they became extensions of his own body. But the greatest gift he was to bring back to Okinawa was the essence of balance.[3] It was a skill that seeped into him slowly, until it ultimately negated his former impulsive manner.

Being endowed of great strength, Yara naturally exulted in activities which demanded collision or body contact. Anything that was a matter of strength or speed evoked the greatest enthusiasm from him. But all the while, his teacher was slowly instilling the value of balance and the principle of harmony.

Each day during his training exercises, his teacher would choose an opportune moment to push him lightly and Yara would stumble to this side or that. No matter how he tried at first, he could not

Anything that was a matter of strength or speed evoked the greatest enthusiasm from him . . . .

maintain his equilibrium.

"All things find their inception in unity," his teacher would softly declare each time Yara would foolishly stumble.

Suddenly one day, it struck him that the "unity" his elder spoke of was that of the mind and the body, and the equilibrium he sought could only be attained after his physical and spiritual parts had achieved an equilibrium of their own.

Before he knew it, 20 years had passed. Time was relative to him now. He remembered his teacher had always said, "Time will be important to the man who has no patience. If he be waiting for a loved one, 10 minutes is a long time. If he be training for perfection, 50 years is just a beginning."

All of this flashed now before Yara's eyes as he sauntered slowly and thoughtfully down the hill. For the first time since he left Okinawa, he felt a lump in his throat. He did not say a word, nor did his teacher behind him. They understood one another perfectly.

At last they came to a quay where the ship lay ready to set sail. His teacher had already made provisions for Yara to be comfortable on the trip, loading all of his worldly belongings, including his bo and twin swords, on board. As the wind filled the sails, Yara stood on deck and watched the distance grow between himself and the shoreline. His last sight of China was his teacher's smiling face.

Okinawa, at this time, was a fiefdom of China and the island depended upon the Emperor of China for military protection as well as commercial trade. Their protection was needed mainly against the pirates who scoured the straits during these times, and against the military ventures of the Satsuma clan from Japan. For the economic good of both countries, China and Japan had come to an agreement over the trade rights in Okinawa. At certain times of the year, the Japanese would come to the island and trade with the Okinawans while the Chinese officials would discreetly stay out of sight and pretend they did not see what was transpiring. The Japanese, for their part, would

. . . . the equilibrium he sought could only be attained after his physical and spiritual parts had achieved an equilibrium of their own.

11

pretend that the Chinese had left the island altogether. During the remainder of the annum, the Chinese would exercise their customary primacy over the islanders.

In this situation, the only ones who lost out were the Okinawans.

If the Japanese committed excesses, which they were wont to do, the Chinese officialdom would not come to the aid of the natives. When the Japanese went back to Japan, they pretended that China did not maintain a fiefdom at the under-belly of their empire.

This is the home to which Yara returned. His parents, although happy, went about their everyday life as though nothing had happened. The only thing which mattered to them was that their son had returned after 20 years of absence.

Yara's brother was the village mayor, and he had plenty of tasks to keep him busy upon his return. Since he could read and write Chinese, Yara became very useful to the merchants and government officials. He was in great demand because of his ability to translate documents and letters. In fact, he was so busy that he had to utilize the small hours of the morning for continuance of his martial arts training.

During the rare moments when Yara had spare time, he would walk along the many beaches and coves near the village. One day while he was occupied with one of these pleasant sojourns, he heard a high-pitched hysterical cry for help. He stopped in his tracks and listened intently. His ears disregarded the constant blowing of the sea breeze and the rhythmic pounding of the surf, and he held his breath.

The screams made their way to his ears again, and in a flash, Yara was sprinting toward the distressful sounds. As he shot over a sand dune, he was astonished to see a samurai struggling with a young girl. The samurai looked upon him, still holding the girl, as Yara strode downhill toward them.

"Why don't you leave the girl alone?" shouted

> .... he heard a high-pitched, hysterical cry for help.

Yara over the sounds of the surf and wind. "If you want a girl, there are plenty in the Aka-sen in Naha."

Yara continued to approach the samurai as he spoke, showing no expression on his face. When he came face to face with the ruffian, he added, "You ought to be ashamed of yourself—a samurai attacking a helpless girl."

The samurai blinked at what he thought was impudence from this stranger. He let go of the girl and turned his body to face Yara, saying, "If you know what is good for you, you will stay out of matters that do not concern you." The girl, suddenly free from the grasp of her attacker, fled to a nearby dune and turned to watch the two men from a distance.

Yara calmly gazed at the samurai, noticing the crest of Satsuma on his kimono. He let his eyes wander to the weapon and noticed the sword was of good quality. The glance was not lost on the samurai, who grasped the sword by the hilt and shifted his body.

Yara instinctively moved back one step and let his hands dangle loosely at his sides. He only realized the delicacy of his weaponless situation when the samurai suddenly drew his sword and advanced.

Yara waited.

For the first time in his life, at the age of 32, Yara found himself in a life or death situation. His training period was over now. It was the real thing. He began to tense as he watched the samurai's cautious approach, and the words of his teacher came back to him: "Unless the mind is calm, it cannot concentrate."

He took a deep breath and relaxed his shoulders. He stepped backward one more time and exhaled, allowing his feelings drop down to his lower abdomen. All of the nervousness was gone now. He was ready to take on the matter at hand.

The samurai slowly moved his sword to a *hasso* position and stopped. Time stood still for a flicker of a second and the samurai struck. The sword swung

The samurai blinked at what he thought was impudence from this stranger.

sideways in a classical *do* cut, but Yara leapt two strides backward, avoided the cut, and circled around until he stood knee-deep in the surf. The angered samurai raced after him, wading clumsily through the salty brine with his sword held high above his head. Yara chose his time carefully, and at the right moment, he retraced his steps back to the beach, further angering the samurai in hot pursuit.

The girl watched Yara come near her with the samurai behind him, and felt helpless. She glanced quickly around her and caught sight of a small boat only a few yards away. Running frantically to the small craft, she grabbed an oar and quickly tossed it to Yara, who was now only a short distance away.

In a split second, Yara had the oar firmly gripped and spun around to face his enemy. The samurai, cursing to himself over having lost his tremendous advantage, stopped and assumed a *jo-dan kamai*.[4] Yara countered this ploy by holding his oar in a *dragon tail kamai*,[5] and for what appeared to be an eternity to the female spectator, the two men faced each other like statues. Only the sound of their throats and chests heaving for air disturbed the eery musical harmony of the wind and the surf.

Suddenly, the samurai struck. Yara's reaction was instantaneous, striking the sword at the hilt with his oar. The blow was perfectly executed, sending the sword skyward, but at the moment of contact, Yara inexplicably jumped upward as though he had anticipated the samurai's next move. This was a dangerous gambit, but it worked. As soon as the Satsuma henchman felt his grip loosen on the hilt of his sword, he immediately squatted to one knee and pulled his short sword.

Yara was in perfect position and took instinctive advantage, unleashing a frighteningly powerful side kick which connected with a sickening thud to the samurai's head. The kick sent him sprawling backward, at the very feet of the girl he had been molesting. Desperately, he tried to raise himself off the ground, but Yara was upon him in an instant,

The kick sent him backward, at the very feet of the girl he had been molesting.

slashing his oar downward and crushing the samurai's skull.

He died without a gasp.

The girl looked around nervously to see if anyone had seen the battle. When she was satisfied that they were alone, she said, "Help me bury him. Don't ask any questions now. You are new here and I will explain later."

Heeding her advice, Yara grasped the still-warm carcass and both of them dragged the body away from the beach and buried it in a clump of bushes.

"If the other samurai find his body with a crushed skull," said the girl breathlessly, "they will take it out on the native Okinawans."

"What if his friends miss him when he does not show up?" queried Yara. "What then?"

"They won't miss him. Most of the samurai who come here are plunderers and the others may think he has gone off to some other locale in search of loot."[6]

"Do you mean to tell me these things take place all of the time?" asked Yara, excited but still winded from his ordeal. "My brother and those of my village did not tell me of such happenings, and I have been back from China now for three months."

. . . both of them dragged the body away from the beach and buried it in a clump of bushes.

The girl looked quizzically at Yara, thinking, "No wonder he is a skilled martial artist. He can probably hold his own against any samurai." This prompted her to compliment him: "You must have trained in the martial arts for a long time. No one I know can match a samurai, no less defeat him in the manner which you have just demonstrated."

"I trained for 20 years in China," answered Yara, "but I did not train for this. I must admit to you, however, that philosophy is not an antidote against the behavior displayed by that samurai."

The girl could no longer contain herself and spoke to Yara in a tone which was somewhere between commanding and beseeching.

"Will you teach your art to our people?" she asked. "These are troubled times and we need to learn how to defend ourselves against outsiders."

Yara, struck by the urgency in her voice, said he would think about it, then led her away from the hasty grave. In 15 minutes, they had come upon a small fishing village.

"This is it," she said. "This is my village. We would be honored by your presence if you should pass this way again. I live at the village headmaster's home." With that, she ran off and left Yara standing alone.

The days which followed were characterized by a germination of the seed she had planted in his head. During his training exercises, he gave serious thought of sharing his knowledge with the local young men. He made it a point of inquiring into the activities of the Japanese traders and samurai who frequented the island. This, after all, was his home.

The more his mind dwelled on the dilemma, the more correct the girl seemed to be. The pirates and plunderers were making life miserable for the natives of Okinawa, his countrymen. One day, his resolve hardened into bold action.

He gradually gathered a few students around him and began to instruct them in his art. As practice was confined to the chilly hours of the morning, his followers were whittled down to but four, two of them—cousins who lived in the same village.

In time, the villagers became accustomed to the sounds which emanated from Yara's house, the kiais and the clacking of stick against stick. When strangers visited the village, Yara's entourage would practice in silence. At this time, his students concentrated mainly on power, even in their kata training, hitting tree trunks and doing only the most rigorous calisthenics.

But regardless of how hard he tried to maintain the secrecy of his classes, word got around. One day while he was translating a document, his maid announced the arrival of a stranger who had come expressly to see him.

"He is not of this village or this part of the country," the maid volunteered, "but he looks strong, and he is apparently a martial artist."

When strangers visited the village, Yara's entourage would practice in silence.

Yara felt himself tighten when he heard this. He went into the courtyard with a certain amount of apprehension and viewed a short, stocky man in his early 20s, sitting on a bench with a pair of sai held in one hand. The stranger stood up politely as Yara approached him.

"Sorry to disturb you," he said, "but are you Chatan-Yara?"

"Yes I am," answered Yara, staring straight into the man's eyes.

"I am from the island of Hama-Higa,"[7] volunteered the stranger. "My name is Shiroma and I have come from my island in hopes that you will teach me proficiency with the sai."

"I do not give lessons without an introduction," said Yara, who smiled and then turned to walk back to his study.

"HOLD IT!!!" shouted the stranger, now beside himself. "I did not come all this way to be turned down. I have traveled extensively, looking for a man who is my superior with the sai. I have met and defeated all so-called masters, and I have come to you knowing that you are supposed to be the greatest in Okinawa. This I heard from the mouth of the village headmaster's daughter. A lesson from you would show me whether or not she spoke the truth."

Yara was surprised at this and could only concern himself with the girl rather than the challenge.

"This headmaster's daughter, was she a slender girl with apple cheeks?"

"Yes," answered the stranger, "it fits the description. In that case, you must truly be the great Chatan-Yara and I did not come in vain."

"Young man," continued Yara, "did you pass through Tsu Ken Shita Haku?"[8]

"Yes, their sai techniques are good, but their sai expert was unfortunately sick and not quite himself."

Yara studied the young man intently. He saw an aura of cocksure vanity and decided to extend him a lesson in humility. His only problem was to find a way to do so without hurting him, for Yara liked the

He saw an aura of cocksure vanity and decided to extend him a lesson in humility.

17

brazen young man and realized that he differed little from so many other young martial artists who relied so heavily on strength and disregarded the mind.

"Meet me at the beach tomorrow morning at daybreak," spat Yara suddenly, "and I will give you a lesson." With this, he retired to his study.

At daybreak the following day, Yara was sitting in deep meditation on the sand, the sun rising in its red fiery brilliance over his shoulder. He felt a blissful harmony with the sky and the earth. Without looking, he was aware of something disturbing this calm from a distance, approaching him steadily. The man who approached him was full of tension and excitement. Yara could feel it, but he waited until the taut form was only about six feet away before he opened his eyes.

"Here I am," said Shiroma, taking his sai from their sling and holding one in each hand. Yara smiled and stood up.

"Are you ready for a lesson?" he asked Shiroma.

The brass youngster responded by assuming a defensive posture. Yara contrived to humiliate the young man from the outset by holding his sai at his sides in a natural stance. Shiroma, sensing that Yara's calm was an indication that he actually was a great master, decided to circle around him toward the sea to obtain the advantage of having the sun at his back. "If I move over enough," he thought, "the sun will strike him in the eyes and blind him to my attack."

Yara continued to smile, following the young man with his eyes.

As Shiroma slowly shuffled in a circle, tense and superlatively alert, his inner voice screamed to him, "Make your move the instant the sun hits his face. Why is the devil so calm? Make your first strike count! There will be no second chance with a man like this."

Shiroma had finally reached a point within one step of getting the sun flush into Yara's eyes. Yara was still facing him with his sai held loosely at his sides, which made the young man very uneasy.

> Shiroma finally reached a point within one step of getting the sun flush into Yara's eyes.

In a flash, Shiroma made his final step, and only then did Yara raise his sai. It was the last thing Shiroma would remember. In fact, he often told the anecdote as he recollected it later: "The moment I moved into position, he raised one sai and used it as a mirror, deflecting the sun's rays into my eyes. He made me a victim of my own gambit. My trap miscarried, and I later awoke in Yara's front room with a throbbing headache and a bump on my head."

Shiroma stayed on to become Yara's student.

The later years of Yara are shrouded in mystery. Most of the studies looking into his life appear to tell us that he spent most of his remaining time in calligraphy and translation. He did not follow through in propagating a school of karate like those who came after him, but he did pass on to us the *Chatan-Yara bo kata* and the *Chatan-Yara sai kata.*[9]

It was the last thing Shiroma would remember.

NOTES FOR YARA

1. Yara was born in the village of Chatan, therefore meriting the name Chatan-Yara. In English it is the equivalent of saying Yara from Chatan.

2. After the year 1392, a great number of Chinese families settled in Okinawa and, through generations, served in important official positions. The Chinese influence lasted until the reign of Emperor Sho Tai (1848-79) and the Okinawans customarily looked to China for their cultural and educational guidance during this time.

3. Yara initiated the concept of inner strength to Okinawan karate, while Miyagi Chojun popularized it with his system of Goju. Miyagi studied Pakua, whereas Yara studied Hsing-I and Chi-kung.

4. Jo-dan kamai: the posture in which one holds the weapon with one or both hands high over the head.

5. Dragon tail kamai: the posture in which one holds the weapon with one or both hands at a forty-five-degree angle to the side of the body and back. Usually, this posture is used by a very skilled martial artist who is not afraid of death, since traditional weapons teachings stress jodan and chudan kamai as safe postures. With the exception of those who have overcome self, most combatants want merely to win and survive.

6. During this era, the legend of the Okinawan secret art was fathered. It gave birth to stories of how the Satsuma samurai took away the weapons of the Okinawans and how the natives responded with an art, now known to us as karate.

7. Hama-Higa: an island off the coast of Okinawa, famous for its sai and tonfa weaponry.

8. Tsu Ken Shita Haku: an Okinawan area famous for sai weaponry. The Tsu Ken Shita Haku sai kata is widely used as a teaching method.

9. Chatan-Yara kata for the bo and the sai are supposed to incorporate fighting techniques unique to Okinawa, encouraging bare-hand fighting as the closing struggle.

Karate Sakugawa

KARATE, AS IT IS TODAY, IS INDEBTED TO A MAN KNOWN AS KARATE SAKUGAWA for a great many things. Among them are the *kushanku* kata,[1] the *Sakugawa bo* kata and the *dojo kun* or gym precept.

He was born in Shuri, Okinawa, March 5, 1733, and died August 17, 1815. When he was 17, his father returned critically ill from a rousting by bullies who had forced him to drink beyond human capacity. Dying, his father said, "Son, take a good look at me. I want you to promise me one thing. Take up the martial arts and don't be like your father. Don't ever let yourself be a subject of ridicule and abuse from bullies and men of that ilk."

After he buried his father, Sakugawa searched for a martial artist and finally heard about a monk named Takahara Peichin,[2] who lived nearby in Akata village. He visited Takahara and explained his mission. Takahara listened to the boy and then said, "The martial arts are a lifetime study. It is not a matter of months or years. It is for life. The philosophical concept is centered around these principles: *do*, a road or way of life, *ho*, law, the performance of kata, and *katsu*, use of the kata in the actual fighting."

Sakugawa went under the wing of Takahara, developed into one of his best students, and the years passed quickly. One day, when he was 23 years old, he decided to visit Nakashima-Yukaku, which was famous for its gay quarters. While crossing a bridge near the Izumizaki inlet, he noticed an elegantly dressed Chinese fellow standing by the edge of the river, watching the reflection of the moon on the water. A sudden mischievous impulse came over Sakugawa. He wanted to push the stranger into the river as a prank. He stealthily crept towards the stranger and suddenly gave a strong push. The Chinese stranger spoke the word, "Danger!" in strongly accented Okinawan, turned and grabbed Sakugawa by the hand in an iron grip.

"Now why did you do that?" the stranger asked. "Do you realize your prank could have resulted in some danger? What if I were some weakling unable to cope with this situation? You are very powerful and you should not play like this. The Okinawan people have been very kind to me and I will overlook this, but refrain from such pranks in the future."

Sakugawa was so ashamed he did not know what to say. At this moment a young man approached them and gave a jug of sake to the Chinese stranger. Turning to Sakugawa, the young man asked, "Are you not Sakugawa? I was not sure whether I had recognized you. What are you doing here?"

"Do you know him?" the Chinese gentleman asked the young man, pointing to Sakugawa.

"Yes," the young man said, "He is a well-known local karate student who shows great promise."

The Chinese gentleman peered intently at Sakugawa. "If you ever come to Kume-mura,[3] ask for Kushanku and I will teach you not only the how, but also the why, of the martial arts." And pointing to the young man who had brought him the jug, he said, "He is Kitani-Yara, a student of mine who is helping me during my stay in this country."

Overwhelmed with emotion at this stroke of luck, Sakugawa could hardly wait to get back to his sensei and tell him of this account. When he related his story, Takahara was also overjoyed and said, "Go to

He wanted to push the stranger into the river as a prank.

Kushanku and learn what you can. He is the most skillful of all the martial artists who have ever come from China. Fortune is smiling on you. When Kushanku returns to China, you are welcome to come back to this house. Now Hurry!"

He followed his advice and stayed for six years with Kushanku. At the age of 29, however, he received an urgent message from his sensei, Takahara, to come back to Shuri. He returned quickly and found his sensei seriously ill. The old man said, "The reason I called you back is because I want you to carry on karate the correct way. After my death, I want you to name yourself Karate Sakugawa and make the Okinawan people proud of you."

Two days later Takahara passed away. When Kushanku returned to China, Sakugawa returned to Shuri and carried on from where Takahara had left off.

He returned quickly and found his sensei seriously ill.

Without reservation, we can say that Sakugawa was the first teacher and master of the style that is commonly called true Okinawan and Japanese karate. The true karate master is a general practitioner well versed in all aspects of the art, and not a specialist in only one aspect.

Specialists exist in all areas of the martial arts. The specialist thrives in his environment. He is a standout by virtue of his expertise in one particular aspect of his art. In judo, there is the *seoinage* specialist, in karate, the side kicker, etc., and the list could go on *ad infinitum*. In sports competition, some martial artists become champions. However, sports is a far cry from desperate combat.

The specialist often cannot distinguish the forest from the trees. He has developed his particular technique, and it has worked for him. His perspective is shrouded by too much attention to a particular technique. He becomes a person who knows more and more about less and less.

Karate Sakugawa had three students who were known as the "Three Musketeers," inseparable buddies named Okuda, Makabe and Matsumoto.[4] They were his assistant instructors and were granted recognition by their admiring public.

Okuda was the specialist supreme. He was the "one-punch" knockout artist and was aptly named "Iron Hand" Okuda.[5] Villagers would say, "Okuda can kill a bull with one blow." Whenever Okuda would visit a village, people would say, "Okuda is coming!" and an admiring throng would quickly gather around him.

Makabe was small. He was quick, clever and elusive in his movements. Legend has it that he moved as if borne on the wings of a bird. He was called "Bird Man" Makabe.[6] People flocked around him also.

Among the three, Matsumoto was the general practitioner. He did all things well, mastered all the basics and had no one specialty. When the "Three Musketeers" walked into town, no one flocked around him. He was not a specialist. Sometimes someone would inquire and say, "Who is that? What is his specialty? What can he do?" And the answer would always be, "Oh, him. He is a good teacher. Nothing special."[7]

One day a ship from China dropped anchor in the harbor of Naha, Okinawa. On board was a ship's captain named Oshima-Kuryu[8] who was a renowned fighter. Oshima-Kuryu, in all his travels, had never been beaten, and he reveled in his prowess. As his ship lay at anchor, Oshima-Kuryu was thinking to himself, "I wonder how I can get someone to fight me? The people here know me and will not accept a challenge. I must come up with something."

One day an idea hit him. That night he went to the town tavern, picked a fight with a town tough and, after beating him, took his clothes as a sign of victory. Following his plan, he repeated the same procedure again and again. After a period of time, the people in Okinawa put in a strong complaint against a Chinese martial artist who took his victim's clothes after beating them. The news came to the town of Shuri, and finally to Karate Sakugawa, who also acted as the peace magistrate, a function of most karate

Oshima-Kuryu, in all his travels, had never been beaten . . . .

masters in those days.

One night Karate Sakugawa's best students, the "Three Musketeers," were walking along a mountain path at the edge of town when a large shadow loomed across their path. They saw a huge person with clothes slung over his shoulder. Instinctively, they knew it was the man about whom they had heard.

Okuda said, "Halt! You there—are you the one who has caused all the commotion in the vicinity of Naha? If you are, turn yourself in or we will force you to do so."

Oshima-Kuryu slowly turned his head and said, "I'll turn myself in if I am beaten. Do you see these clothes? I have taken them from experts like yourselves."

Okuda charged like a bull and threw his famous punch, but Kuryu side-stepped. As hard as Okuda tried, he could not land his punch and finally, after he was winded, Kuryu knocked him down. Kuryu said, "Tomorrow night I shall be here at the same time."

> They saw a huge person with clothes slung over his shoulder.

The next night, Makabe the "Bird Man" was waiting. Kuryu appeared, and they fought. Makabe was quick and fast, clever and cunning. But it was not enough. Kuryu met his every maneuver and finally, after wearing Makabe down, Kuryu won the fight.

The town people heard the news and were worried. They all beseeched Karate Sakugawa to take care of Oshima-Kuryu himself. But Sakugawa said, "Do not worry. Our two specialists have failed. They failed to see very obvious things because they were too intent with their own specialties. Matsumoto has grown in breadth from specialist to general practitioner. He will prevail."

Matsumoto faced Oshima-Kuryu on the third night. When they squared off, Oshima-Kuryu realized he was facing his most formidable opponent to date. They fought for a long time without a sound. Finally, Oshima-Kuryu attacked with his last ounce of strength. Matsumoto faded away, and before Oshima-Kuryu knew what had happened, Matsumoto came up from the side and knocked him down.

"The time has come for me to retire," Oshima-Kuryu later said. "I'm glad that I was beaten by a man who has mastered the basics. All my previous opponents were specialists. They all had a gimmick, but it was not enough."

When Sakugawa retired, he passed on his *menkyo-kaiden*[9] to Matsumoto. However, his greatest achievement came when he was 78 years old. It was then that Sokon Matsumura came to him for lessons.

NOTES FOR KARATE SAKUGAWA

1. At present, there are several versions of the kushanku kata, depending on the school. In English, they are sometimes written as "kusanku" and in Japanese, it is pronounced "koshokun."

2. Peichin: a feudal title given to a samurai by his king for distinguishing services rendered.

3. Kumemura (Toei): an area near Naha, Okinawa, where Chinese families from the Fukien coast had settled. These families were carefully chosen by the Chinese Emperor to facilitate relations between Okinawa and the Chinese court.

4. Genwa Nakasone, *Karate-Do, Daikan,* (Tokyo, 1954), p. 205.

5. Ibid., p. 206.

6. Ibid.

7. Ibid.

8. Ibid., p. 207.

9. Menkyo-kaiden: a certificate of full proficiency in an art, usually given to a student deemed most suited to carry on the art of his sensei. A master customarily issued only one menkyo-kaiden in his lifetime.

. . . . his greatest achievement came when he was 78 years old.

Sakugawa No Kon & Others

T HE GREATEST SINGLE INFLUENCE ON THE HISTORY OF OKINAWAN KARATE came during the Ming Dynasty (1368-1644), for it was during this period that the art of the *bo* (staff) was refined and handed down to us. The Chinese terminology for the bo is *kon* and it is still used to describe a bo kata. For example, Sakugawa no kon means Sakugawa bo kata.

The Okinawans and Japanese used different types of oak and iron to make their bo. Some were: *kashiwagi-bo* or Mongolian oak, *kashiki-bo* or oak (red or white), *kana-bo*, *kurogane-bo*, *tetsu-no-bo* or iron, *kunugi-no-bo* or silkworm oak.

Karate Sakugawa, who was born in Shuri-Akata, Okinawa, went to China and refined his art. He gave us the *Sakugawa no kon*. A teacher in the real tradition of the Chinese, he was secretive about his kata and did not teach them to anyone until he felt that he could trust them to someone who could be his successor.

Sakugawa's top student in the bo was a man by the name of Ginowan Donchi. Ginowan studied his sensei's every move from the time his sensei woke up to the time his sensei went to bed. Dogging his sensei's footsteps, Ginowan was able to watch Sakugawa practice the bo secretly.

One day Sakugawa spied Ginowan practicing and

realized that Ginowan somehow must have watched him in action. On the spot, Sakugawa decided that Ginowan would carry on his art with the bo, sai and other weapons.

In time, Ginowan developed his kata to a degree equal to, or better than, his teacher. The result was the *Ginowan no kon*.

Another famous master of the bo who lived several hundred years ago was a man by the name of Sueishi. He developed the *Cho-Un no kon*.

Sueishi did not teach many people and for long periods of time would train by himself. Sometimes the duration of his inactivity, as far as teaching was concerned, stretched into months, and all entreaties from eager, prospective students were to no avail.

Sueishi had a very faithful servant named Chinen Shichanaka. Chinen, who knew his master well, went about his duties, seemingly uninterested in the martial arts. However, Chinen kept his eyes open and whenever his master practiced with the bo, he made sure that somehow his duties found him near the practice sight.

> . . . Sakugawa decided that Ginowan would carry on his art . . . .

One day, Sueishi noticed that his servant was busy doing some work while he was practicing the bo. Sueishi suddenly realized that Chinen was always working in the area when he was with his bo.

Sueishi called to Chinen, "I notice that you are around or seem to have something to do whenever I am practicing with my bo. Why?"

"Because I want to learn your bo and your art, but I am only a servant. I could not ask you to teach me so my only hope was to watch you practice."

When Sueishi realized that Chinen was serious, he taught him his art. As a result, Chinen developed a bo kata, the *Chinen Shichanaka no kon*, as we know it today.

Many of the Okinawan weapon kata come from islands in the Okinawan chain such as Yaeyama and Hama-Higa. For instance, the *Akahachi no gyaku bo* of Oyake Akahachi (who was a bo *meijin* and a legend in his time) came down from Yaeyama island. He was famous for reverse techniques and the mastery of his kata enabled one to subdue opponents as well as destroy them.

Some bo masters went to China as Sakugawa did, and perfected their art there. Miyazato was one of them. Unlike the others, however, Miyazato retained the Chinese influence and his bo kata, *Miyazato no kon*, reflects the Chinese movements. Some who have seen this bo kata will swear that it is Chinese and not Okinawan.

Tsuken Hantaka, a weapons master, studied extensively in Yaeyama and it is said that his bo art truly represents reverse techniques.

The *Sueyoshi no kon* is still extensively used today in Okinawa but details of who Sueyoshi was and where he studied are not available.

. . . . his contribution to the art was narrow and specialized.

Nakanhari, who gave us the *Nakanhari no kon*, lived less than a hundred years ago. As a legendary bo expert, his contribution to the art was narrow and specialized. Sometimes during festivals in Okinawa his bo kata is shown to the public, but it is not often practiced by karate enthusiasts.

Chinen of Yamane Ryu no Chinen Sensei contributed most of the popular bo kata taught today. Chinen studied under many masters and taught karate experts Oshiro Choki and Yabiku Moden. They passed on to us the following katas: *Shiu-Shi no kon*, *Shirotaru no kon, and Yonegawa no kon.*

"Bushi" Matsumura passed on the *Matsumura no kon*. Not many have knowledge of this kata and, although some claim to use this kata, it is probably a bastardized version of the true form.

Toyama founded the Toyama school of *Bo jutsu* and developed the *Toyama no kon*. Unfortunately for Toyama, he did not pursue his art further than the bo, and only students of the bo would come across his style. It is comparatively unknown to the average karate practitioner.

The following bo kata are the most popular today and can be seen in the dojo of Okinawa, Japan, and wherever karate is taught in other parts of the globe:

SAKUGAWA NO KON AND OTHERS

* Sakugawa no kon
* Shiu-Shi no kon
* Cho-Un no kon
* Shirotaru no kon
* Yonegawa no kon
* Chinen Shichanaka no kon
* Sesoku no kon
* Urasoe no kon
* Sueyoshi no kon
* Sueishi no kon

* Arakaki no kon
* Chatan-Yara no kon

*　　*　　*　　*

On the following pages, Mr. Robert Leong performs excerpts from the opening of the Sakugawa no Kon bo kata. Mr. Leong is a former kata champion and a student of the author.

Bushi Matsumura

I
T WAS ONLY A SHORT TIME AFTER A CORSICAN-BORN ITALIAN of impoverished nobility named Napoleone Buonaparte had grasped Europe by the throat that, on the other side of the globe, Sofuku Matsumura was making entreaties for his son's martial arts education. Sofuku made a pilgrimage to see a 78-year-old gentleman named Karate Sakugawa, bringing his most sturdily built son, Sokon.

"Let me see the boy," rasped the old master with eccentric body quivers.

The boy was brought forward, feeling self-conscious and slightly afraid, until he stood before the strange old man.

"Sokon," the old man addressed him sternly, "to take up the martial arts is to take up a new way of life. You will soon find that your character and personality are more significant than your physical strength and ability. Do you believe that you will be dedicated enough to succeed?"

Sokon Matsumura, although only in his early teens, stiffened during the old man's probing question and looked around him when the old master finished, as though he were waiting for permission to address him directly.

"I will not disappoint you," he said at length.

Such went Matsumura's first step along the path of

his destiny and eventual fame among the immortals of karate. It was a significant event which ultimately led to the spawning of masters like Itosu, Chinen, Tawata, Yasuzato and Arakaki, and the systematized karate in Shuri and the Sho-Rin ryu.[1]

Once under the tutelage of Sakugawa, Bushi (samurai) Matsumura developed quickly into a proficient martial expert. By the winter of 1816, he was deemed valuable enough to be recruited into imperial service as a *chikudon*[2], allowing him to feel secure enough to marry two years later. Her name was Yonamine Chiru, noted by all who knew her as a remarkably talented and strong woman. She came from a family that was renowned for its karate skills, giving her the proper background to become a major influence in the life of her husband.

As will always happen, tongues started wagging about the marital pairing of the two and Yonamine was rumored to be so strong that she could lift a bag of rice with her left hand while sweeping beneath it with her right. "Who is the more skillful fighter?" was the question most often posed about Matsumura and his wife.

These fires were stoked one night following a party at Kaki-no-hana in Naha. The spirits were flowing freely and the party began to get boisterous, at which point Matsumura told his wife to go home. It was beginning to get dark while Yonamine made her way home along a dirt path. She decided to stop briefly at the Sogen-Ji (temple), but a sudden rustle of the bushes caused her to feel a rush of shock. She spun to the side, only to find three shabbily dressed and unshaven men staring at her with the intense, malicious look of predators with a bead drawn on their prey.

She took half a breath and composed herself, stepping backward at once to an area which was more heavily thicketed.

"Get out of the way, or I shall have to chastise all of you," she said, intending to provoke them.

Her ploy was not lost on the ruffians, who laughed

"Get out of the way, or I shall have to chastise all of you," she said . . . .

and suddenly followed the lead of the man on the right, who began to walk stealthily toward her. Yonamine felt that the bearded one on the right was the leader, and she concentrated on him first. Rather than wait for him to draw any nearer, she set upon him like a cat. There was a flicker of surprise, and even, perhaps, fear in his eyes as he watched grim resolve distort the beautiful woman's face to that of a raging beast with nostrils flared and lips curled back to show her tightly clenched teeth.

Her kiai was powerful and primal as she lunged for him, landing on her right foot and spinning almost a full turn on it. She felt the heel of her other foot slam into some point on the man's face, a perfectly executed spinning heel kick. With hardly a wasted motion, Yonamine leaned to the other side and kicked out sideways as soon as her other foot touched ground. The side kick sank deep into the gut of the man in the center, causing him to slump to the ground in a tiny pile, clawing and gasping for breath. Yet, before his knees had even begun to buckle, Yonamine had straightened up to neutralize her first victim, striking powerfully backward into his throat with the point of her elbow.

Her kiai was powerful and primal as she lunged for him . . . .

The third man, as yet untouched, stopped in his tracks when he witnessed the rapid carnage of his compatriots. He showed her a sickly expression of surprise before he turned in a panic and began to run away. It took Yonamine only three long running strides before she grasped him by the back of his collar, drove her foot into the back of his knee and fell down on top of him. The dry leaves rustled beneath them as she mercifully neutralized him with a snapping backfist strike to his temple.

She dragged the three together, two of them still semi-conscious, back-to-back, and tied them with her obi (wide sash). As an extra measure of her anger, she ripped off the temple inscription pole and laid it on them.

A few hours later, Matsumura was following the identical trail on his way home. As he walked past the temple, he heard movement in the brush and sounds that resembled groaning. Peering into the darkness of the thicket, he was surprised to see three men tied up like cattle, one of them badly beaten with swollen and discolored marks on his face. He untied them and recognized the obi.

At breakfast the following morning, Matsumura flung the sash onto the table in front of his wife and said, "I believe this belongs to you."

His wife, in the midst of cleaning up, took the obi without a word, and went on about her business. Matsumura had been calm about what he had seen up to this point, as though he were waiting for some explanation, some indication that it really wasn't his own sweet wife who manhandled three bandits. He now felt a dizzying rush which started in his stomach and raced to his head. It was true then, what they said about Yonamine's fighting ability. He could hardly keep his pride in check, coming to a firm conclusion that he will have to one day find out for himself.

> The stunned Matsumura had no time to catch himself . . . .

That day came not long afterward. Yonamine's relatives were holding a large celebration and, feigning sickness, Matsumura stayed behind. Shortly before dark, he dressed himself as a farmer, rubbed his face with charcoal and hurried to Daido Matsubara, a spot he knew his wife would have to pass on her way home. Hidden in a hedgerow, he watched his wife merrily treking down the road, swinging a *furoshiki*[3] in her left hand. At what he believed to be the right moment, he pounced out upon her with a thundering kiai, hoping only to knock her down. Her reaction was spontaneous. She dropped the furoshiki and jumped straight into the air, connecting with kicks to two different parts of his torso before she again landed. The stunned Matsumura had no time to catch himself, for within the second, he felt the prominent back knuckles of his own wife's hand thudding across his skull. He was then only dimly aware that she was tying him to a tree.

Matsumura was crestfallen, helpless to free himself

during the entire night. When the first rays of dawn began to warm him, a horseman approached him aboard a black trotting steed.

"Over here," shouted Matsumura. "Untie me!"

The horseman dismounted and stiffened when he noticed that it was the great Matsumura in such a position.

"I know," he said, self-conscious and somewhat ashamed, "You are wondering what happened. I'm wondering myself. Just leave it to rest that the world is a large place, and I have discovered there can be more skillful martial artists than myself in it."

Now, like a dog with his tail between his legs, he returned home. His sweet wife smiled at the tale when he told her a fabrication about the scores of men who set upon him during a walk. Serving him his breakfast, she remarked, "You should be more careful and train harder."

Matsumura could wait no later than that very evening to see his sensei, old Sakugawa. The aged man giggled after hearing his story and finally decided to give him some advice.

"My student, where is your most vulnerable area? A woman's breast is akin to it in sensitivity. They will go to great lengths trying to prevent a blow from landing there. The next time you encounter a woman who is a strong martial artist, fake a strike at her breast and she will lose composure. If she happens to be stronger than a man, hit her there."

Matsumura, totally deflated after his defeat at the hands of his wife, clung to this bit of advice and waited for still another opportunity to defeat her. It came in two months, for she went off alone to visit her home in Yonbara, some distance away from Shuri. While waiting for sundown, Matsumura dressed himself as a fisherman, rubbing himself with oil and pigmentation so he would look sunburned. He chose his spot along the road and waited.

It was not long after the sun went down that his wife walked past him. Matsumura jumped out at her with his kiai, as before, only this time he kept his

While waiting for sundown, Matsumura dressed himself as a fisherman .

distance. Yonamine stepped back and began to circle him, crouching like a cat ready to pounce. He made an excellent faked punch attempt toward her breast area, which caused her so much consternation that he was able to move in, grasp her and throw her to the ground with an *osoto-gari*. Yonamine was stunned but not hurt, and her husband took the opportunity to run home, wash himself and pretend he was drinking.

"Omedeto gozaimasu," she said enthusiastically as she finally entered their home.

"Why omedeto," asked Matsumura, pretending not to know what she was talking about, "What have I done to receive this congratulation?"

"Tonight you have arrived," she said, sitting down at the table with a smile. "You see, I knew it was you all along tonight and the last time. Karate Sakugawa has finally taught you how to cope with any type of adversary, even a woman. You have learned a valuable lesson, my husband, that in combat you should not distinguish between the sexes. An opponent is an opponent. Sometimes, as you may have learned, a woman can be much more dangerous than a man for that very reason. I am happy for you."

* * * *

Yonamine stepped back and began to circle him, crouching like a cat ready to pounce.

In the years of maturation to come, Matsumura distinguished himself time and again with valorous and heroic deeds. In a relatively short period of time, he became legendary, not only in Okinawa, but in Japan and China as well. His king finally saw fit to award him with the official title of "bushi." No martial artist before nor since has been awarded this accolade. Tales of his deeds still exist in amazing numbers, and to attempt to relate all of them would require a volume in itself. It would be interesting, however, for us to deal with a couple of the deeds which contributed to his honorable title of bushi.

One incident occurred during his youth in 1822. He had been moon-gazing during a stroll on the open road near Nami-no-ue, still feeling the euphoric effects of the sake he had been drinking. Yet, his quick reflexes were not dulled to the point where he could not react quickly when a hooded figure suddenly materialized from the bushes. Matsumura leapt to the side, away from the attacker, and the two began to circle one another cautiously. In a flash of movement almost too quick to see, the hooded attacker hurled a sai at Matsumura, who had to throw his body to the ground in order to avoid it. He rolled twice and shot back to his feet, determined now to destroy this stranger, who was obviously a good martial artist. Matsumura carefully drew a *tessen*, which was fastened to his obi and watched his opponent for the right moment. The hooded man was grunting, and he held his remaining sai before him at chest level.

Matsumura now held his tessen in a *jodan-kamae*, and just as the hooded man lunged at his throat with the sai, Matsumura instinctively executed a *tai-sabaki*, hitting the attacker across the wrist with the weapon. The sai was flung from the attacker's grasp by the blow, and the hooded man was so shocked by the turn of events that he fled. Matsumura picked up the sai and examined it. Some years later, he learned that it belonged to a Chinese martial artist who had returned to China following his defeat at the hands of Matsumura.[4]

> In a flash of movement almost too quick to see, the hooded attacker hurled a sai . . . .

* * * *

Another very famous and oft-repeated story also played a large part in earning Matsumura the title of bushi. It took place during the reign of king Sho Ko, a reign which was marked by court intrigues, corruption and distribution of the king's power into the hands of a small group of his subordinates. It was a familiar story in the history of man, seeming to occur whenever a weak-willed but well-meaning king stepped to the throne.

To keep the people's outrage over rising taxes to a minimum, the king instituted an annual event of bullfighting and martial arts to entertain the populace. It soon became one of the high points of the year.

One particular year, after the king had received a bull from the Emperor of Japan, he decided to match it against his best martial artist, Matsumura. The proclamation of the match went all over the island, creating a great deal of excitement. The people forgot their problems and anxiously anticipated the pitting of Matsumura against the king's bull at Aizo-Shuri.

On hearing of his matching by royal decree, Matsumura decided to take no chances. He made his way to the king's stables and visited the bullkeeper in his home. The man was utterly speechless when he saw the form of Matsumura, a man idolized by the Okinawans as being godlike. He could only stare with his eyes transfixed, his breath held and his mouth held agape.

"Can I see the bull?" asked Matsumura, making an attempt to relax the man.

"Anything you say," uncomfortably responded the bullkeeper at long last, and began to lead Matsumura to the bullpen.

"If you will, please do not mention to anyone that I have come to see the animal," said Matsumura, "and be sure that he is tethered down firmly."

From out of his sleeve, he produced a long needle . . . .

The bullkeeper looked at him strangely and nodded in the affirmative as he watched Matsumura don his battle gear and a mask. Looking first to see that the bull was well tethered, Matsumura then entered the compound and approached the animal cautiously. From out of his sleeve, he produced a long needle, and with it, he jabbed the bull in the nose. The reaction was stunning. The bull bellowed and tried in vain to attack his tormentor.

Matsumura, satisfied with the results, repeated this process every single day until the bull learned to recognize and fear him.

When the day of the match finally came, people flocked to the arena from all over the island and even as far away as Hama-Higa. The air was filled with festivity and people forgot about their taxes. Instead, they prepared themselves for the greatest spectacle on earth: Matsumura fighting the prize bull.

When the bull finally trotted out into the arena, there was an expectant hush and a collective gasp of awe. He was truly a magnificent animal. Even the king must have wondered if any human being could be a match for such a beast.

The bull pawed the ground and snorted ferociously as a cheer gradually worked its way around the arena from one of its corners. Matsumura had appeared. He walked slowly toward the bull, dressed in his battle gear and mask. But when the bull finally caught his scent, he gave a bellow of fear and ran out of the arena.

A great roar went up from the crowd. No one there had ever seen or heard of such a thing. The king himself was speechless, wondering how Matsumura made the bull run without ever having touched it. When he finally regained his composure, he announced to the crowd, "Today, Matsumura is named by royal decree, 'bushi', in recognition of his unusual ability in the martial arts."

The bull pawed the ground and snorted ferociously . . . .

Sokon Matsumura thus carried the name of "bushi" into history.

*   *   *   *

One additional incident, which occurred after he received the honored title, helped to strengthen Matsumura's reputation as a psychologist as well as a great martial artist. It began innocently enough one day, while Matsumura had taken his tobacco pipe to a craftsman in order to have a certain type of carving made on it. This particular craftsman, Uehara, happened to be a karate expert of some note, considered to be the equal of just about anyone in the art. Since Uehara did not belong to any particular school, he could engage in all sorts of combat without fear of recrimination from a sensei. At this time, he was in his early 40s and was aptly named Karate-No-Uehara.[5]

He looked up as Matsumura entered his shop, resting his eyes upon a man much younger than himself, standing tall for an Okinawan at about 5-feet, 9-inches.

"You are Matsumura sensei," declared the crafts-man, paying no attention to the younger man's inquiry about his tobacco pipe.

"Yes."

"I want a favor from you first," continued Uehara, quite without respect. "Do not worry about the pipe, as it is as good as done. I wish to know if you will grant me the pleasure for which I have waited a long time—I want a lesson from you, Matsumura."

The bushi had been anxious about this before he had even entered the shop. He tried to beg off apologetically, but Uehara persisted.

"Are you not the king's instructor?" he asked. "Don't tell me you are afraid to give me a few lessons."

"Yes, I am the king's instructor. I instruct him and no one else. It is for this reason alone that I cannot work with you."

Uehara looked at him with disdain, saying, "Make an exception this time, sensei, and I will challenge you to a match."

Matsumura had decided that this fellow deserved a lesson in common courtesy. He didn't know how he would go about it without actually breaking his bond as the king's personal instructor, but he had come to a definite decision.

"All right, Uehara-san. I will honor your chal-lenge."

Uehara told him to be in a certain spot in the king's graveyard at precisely five o'clock the next morning.

Early that morning, Uehara decided he would get a jump on the bushi. He arrived at the graveyard an hour before time in order to familiarize himself with the terrain, pinpoint the slippery spots and thereby gain an advantage. The graveyard was filled with a thick mist along the side of a green hill, obscuring even the nearby grave markers in the chilly predawn light. Uehara felt a shiver of discomfort as he climbed the small hill to the top, as though he were once again a child and susceptible to fits of an overactive

41

imagination. He retained this eerie disposition as he reached the top of the hill, where the mist was considerably thinner. Suddenly, he heard something that set his heart pounding so loudly that he nearly passed out.

"Uehara," said the baritone voice, "I have been waiting."

The craftsman completely lost his composure and spun wildly in the direction of the sound. From out of the misty shroud stepped Matsumura, a spectre of fearsome proportions. He had outsmarted Uehara, being sure to arrive even earlier. This was not lost on the craftsman, who now gritted his teeth knowing that Matsumura had the advantage of knowing the terrain.

"Are you ready, Uehara?" added the bushi, still walking slowly forward in an ominous manner.

Random and panicked thoughts began to rush through Uehara's mind.

Without speaking, Uehara jumped back into his kamae, while Matsumura stood watching him calmly, his hands remaining at his sides. Random and panicked thoughts began to rush through Uehara's mind. He was plainly losing his nerve. In desperation, he attacked with a loud kiai, caught sight of the self-assured look in the eyes of Matsumura and promptly stopped short. He then jumped back, his mind now racing, and tried desperately to get a hold of himself. He viewed Matsumura, still standing in the same pose, his determined features etched out of the shadows by the morning light.

"Uehara," said Matsumura in his calm baritone, "do something."

The craftsman circled for a better position and tried to regain some of his composure. Suddenly on the spur of the moment, Uehara made one last desperate attempt. He shouted and began to lunge at Matsumura, but the sight of the bushi's eyes brought forth images of terrible superhuman things, like Fudo-Miyo.[6] Uehara's body would not obey the desperate commands of his mind. He simply fell to his knees and began to sob, totally defeated.

"Do not feel ashamed," advised Matsumura, "you

badly wanted to win. You could taste it in your mouth. But it was your only thought, and it defeated you."

So, saying this, Matsumura left the craftsman to himself. It was a lesson that the bushi tried to pass on to posterity. He cautioned all followers of karate that hunger for glory and vanity alone, would end in defeat. This is perhaps one of the most significant contributions made by Sokon Matsumura.

NOTES FOR BUSHI MATSUMURA

1. Prior to this period, karate was not systematized as we know it. It was generically called kara-te or to-de (Tang Hand). The various styles of kara-te were simply named after each master who taught his own interpretation of the art. Matsumura, however, called his style sho-rin ryu (young forest style). This style should not be confused with the sho-rin ryu (pine forest style) which exists today in Okinawa with a different geneology. The English spelling of the two Japanese words does not point out the differences between the two arts.

2. Chikudon: a position below Satonushi. (See Notes on Karate Sakugawa.)

3. Furoshiki: a cloth wrapper commonly used to carry a variety of goods.

4. Chinese martial artist. A number of stories purport that Matsumura later befriended this man and learned some sai and Chinese kata from him.

5. Karate-No-Uehara: was nicknamed "Karate" because of his martial skills and his propensity for challenging other martial artists.

6. Fudo-Miyo: the name of one of the statue figurines which guard Oriental Buddhist temples.

It was a lesson the bushi tried to pass on to posterity.

Matsumura Patsai

ATSAI (BASSAI IN JAPAN) MEANS TO BREACH or go through fortifications, producing the connotation that this kata has the ability to split any defense.

Illustrations may give some idea of the kata, but pictures alone are not enough—it must be put into practice, and this is where the need arises for a good sensei, a person who can communicate and motivate his students to practice. For those without a teacher, who has knowledge of the Matsumura Patsai, the operational part of translating the illustrations into practice should be based on one's own knowledge and experience. One must learn to feel the kata.

There is also the danger of improvisation of a kata. To be a true patsai practitioner one must know the Matsumura Patsai—and all movements must be mastered.

Whenever I practice kata, one of my teacher's favorite stories comes to my mind: "One day a student of archery was practicing by himself in the dojo. He thought, "I shall eliminate the first movement—that of stretching the hand upward prior to pulling the bow—and just shoot the arrows as fast as I can. The sensei is not in the dojo now, and he cannot insist that I perform all the movements as he always does. He is such a stickler on the complete kata. I'm glad that he is not here. The kata is not really that important."

The student took two arrows and shot them as fast as he could, eliminating the first movement of the kata. He hit the bullseye, and the student was pleased with himself. As he was congratulating himself, his sensei, who had been in the library adjoining the dojo, came in and admonished the student for eliminating the first movement.

The sensei, a Zen master, knew what the student had done without being in the dojo. The sensei told him, "Practice must be maintained the same at all times, even if no one is watching or supervising. One must practice for one's self. You are not practicing for me or society, you are practicing for yourself—for your self-improvement and total awareness. If you eliminate or add movements to the kata, you are cheating yourself, not me."

It takes great faith, tenacity, and hard work to master a kata. It ought to be studied seriously. This is the true martial spirit.

*   *   *   *

Excerpts from the Matsumura Patsai are performed on the following pages by Rosamund Siani, who has won a number of kata championships, including the All America Karate Federation Women's black belt kata division in 1973, in the Nationals held at Portland, Oregon.

> The student took two arrows and shot them as fast as he could.

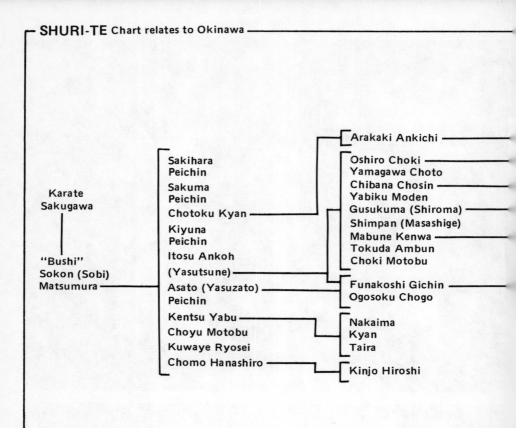

Karate
Sakugawa

"Bushi"
Sokon (Sobi)
Matsumura

- Sakihara Peichin
- Sakuma Peichin
- Chotoku Kyan
- Kiyuna Peichin
- Itosu Ankoh (Yasutsune)
- Asato (Yasuzato) Peichin
- Kentsu Yabu
- Choyu Motobu
- Kuwaye Ryosei
- Chomo Hanashiro

- Arakaki Ankichi
- Oshiro Choki
- Yamagawa Choto
- Chibana Chosin
- Yabiku Moden
- Gusukuma (Shiroma)
- Shimpan (Masashige)
- Mabune Kenwa
- Tokuda Ambun
- Choki Motobu
- Funakoshi Gichin
- Ogosoku Chogo
- Nakaima
- Kyan
- Taira
- Kinjo Hiroshi

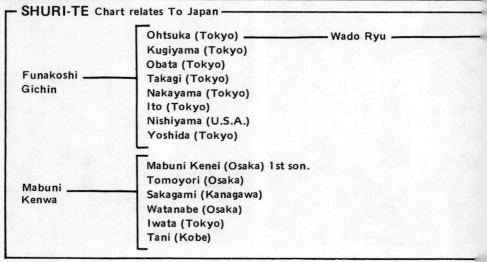

Funakoshi Gichin

- Ohtsuka (Tokyo) ——— Wado Ryu
- Kugiyama (Tokyo)
- Obata (Tokyo)
- Takagi (Tokyo)
- Nakayama (Tokyo)
- Ito (Tokyo)
- Nishiyama (U.S.A.)
- Yoshida (Tokyo)

Mabuni Kenwa

- Mabuni Kenei (Osaka) 1st son.
- Tomoyori (Osaka)
- Sakagami (Kanagawa)
- Watanabe (Osaka)
- Iwata (Tokyo)
- Tani (Kobe)

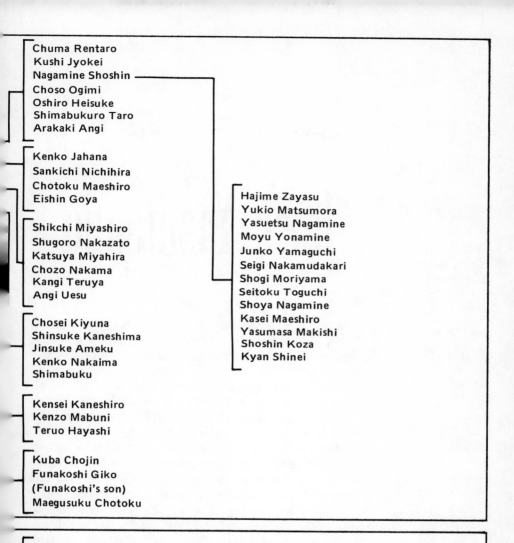

Chuma Rentaro
Kushi Jyokei
Nagamine Shoshin
Choso Ogimi
Oshiro Heisuke
Shimabukuro Taro
Arakaki Angi

Kenko Jahana
Sankichi Nichihira
Chotoku Maeshiro
Eishin Goya

Shikchi Miyashiro
Shugoro Nakazato
Katsuya Miyahira
Chozo Nakama
Kangi Teruya
Angi Uesu

Chosei Kiyuna
Shinsuke Kaneshima
Jinsuke Ameku
Kenko Nakaima
Shimabuku

Kensei Kaneshiro
Kenzo Mabuni
Teruo Hayashi

Kuba Chojin
Funakoshi Giko
(Funakoshi's son)
Maegusuku Chotoku

Hajime Zayasu
Yukio Matsumora
Yasuetsu Nagamine
Moyu Yonamine
Junko Yamaguchi
Seigi Nakamudakari
Shogi Moriyama
Seitoku Toguchi
Shoya Nagamine
Kasei Maeshiro
Yasumasa Makishi
Shoshin Koza
Kyan Shinei

Eriguchi (Tokyo)
Sato
Horiguchi
Suzuki

NOTE:
In Japan proper different ryus sprung up from the karate that the Okinawan masters brought to the mainland; namely, Shotokan and Wado Ryu from the Funakoshi geneology and Shito-Ryu from the Mabuni geneology.

Itosu Yasutsune

BORN IN SHURI NO TŌBARU IN THE YEAR 1830, Itosu Yasutsune achieved, in his 85 years of life, what most karateka can only dream about. He was a *meijin*.[1]

He began his long journey to this ultimate stage of proficiency in the martial arts at an early age. When he was as young as seven years old, his father tied him to a pole with an obi, leaving a free play of about two feet for the boy to run around the pole. His father then took another pole and started to jab him with it. Bewildered, the boy tried to catch the pole with his hands, and not succeeding, ran around the pole until there was no more slack in the obi. His father continued to poke, and the boy, unable to avoid the attack, started to cry. The father did not let up, however. Only when the boy tried desperately to get at his father in anger, did he stop his poking.

Itosu's father continued this process every day until he was satisfied the small boy had developed what he termed a "fighting spirit." "A harsh and drastic means no doubt, but it is in a harsh and drastic climate in which the boy has to take root and grow up into manhood befitting the son of a samurai," he thought.

In 1846, when Sho Iku was king of Okinawa, young Itosu accompanied his father on a visit to bushi Matsumura, who was then 54. After the usual

formal greetings, Itosu's father requested that Matsumura take in his son as a deshi.

Matsumura looked at the young lad, wrinkled his
forehead, and said, "You look thin and at first
appearance, I would say that the martial arts are not
for you. But there is a look in your eyes that I like.
Remember this, attitude is important, the road is
difficult and the most tremendous effort is required."

Itosu nodded his head and kept on looking at the
great Matsumura.

The lessons started the following day. From the
beginning, Itosu never missed a day. There was no
rest. Matsumura scolded, tormented, led, taught,
punished and demanded unconditional submission
and obedience, and soon the 16-year-old boy grew up
into a 24-year-old man. His physique had filled out,
and he had become the tallest man in Shuri.

Sho Tai was now king of Okinawa. Sho Iku, who
had been king when Itosu first started with Matsumura, was in the custody of Japan.[2]

One day, Itosu decided to journey to Naha-shi,
Azamito, hoping to get there while the bull fighting
games were still in progress. As he approached Naha
city, he encountered a wild commotion in the
distance, and he was amazed to see a large bull
running loose and coming toward him at full gallop.

"Run, run for your life," he heard from an excited
chorus of voices in the crowd. "The bull is mad and
has broken out of the compound. He will kill you!"

Yet, Itosu continued walking calmly down the hill,
directly into the path of the charging bull. Many
people in the crowd later remembered a wide grin on
his face as he walked toward certain death.

The bull charged him with his head hung low.
Itosu sidestepped the wild beast and grabbed it
around the horns as it passed. Not a single sound was
uttered from those in the crowd who had not turned
away in fear. They simply watched Itosu run
alongside the tiring beast, turning his head upward by
the horns until it lost its balance and fell to the
ground. When the dust from the fall of man and beast

Itosu nodded
his head and kept
on looking at the
great Matsumura.

finally settled, the crowd was amazed to see Itosu maintaining his vice-like grip on the bull's head. The beast bellowed and squirmed on the ground, but it could not free itself from his grip. At long last, several youths took the opportunity to tie up the panting animal and lead it away.

The excitement of the bull fights that followed was lessened by Itosu's brave act. and afterwards, there was open speculation as to how he would fare against the best martial artists Naha had to offer.[3]

At that particular time in Naha city, there was a huge rock in front of Yamagataya. This rock was called Ude-kake-shi, and it represented a challenge area, a spot where one could issue challenges and fight to prove supremacy in the martial arts.[4] If anyone wanted to gain fame, all he had to do was go to Ude-kake-shi and rest his arm on the rock, symbolizing his willingness to fight. The strong would quickly gather when word was out that someone dared put his arm on the rock, and the challenges would come swift and fast.

Up until that time, the champion was Naha-no-Tomoyose, a strong man and the undefeated idol of Naha city. But in the year 1856, the unbearable humidity drove Itosu to Naha-no-Naminoue to escape the heat where unbeknownst to him, he would find his destiny.

He sat against a huge rock upon his arrival there and began to doze off until he heard some arguing voices carried by the sea breeze.

"Shuri cannot produce a man to defeat Naha's Tomoyose. Their karate is for show and nothing more," said one voice. "In Naha, we produce martial artists for the field—not for the parlor."

"You're right," agreed another. "If it were not for bushi Matsumura, shuri karate would have nothing!"

Itosu decided to do something about this talk, which was hurting his pride. He stood up and suddenly addressed the group, saying, "I think I can prove you gentlemen wrong about shuri karate and your beloved Tomoyose. If you will simply tell me

. . . . the crowd was amazed to see Itosu maintaining his vice-like grip on the bull's head.

how I can go about challenging him, I would be happy to show all of you how 'parlor room' karate fares in the field."

With a degree of repressed glee and excitement, they gave Itosu his wish.

The following day, Itosu went to Naha and approached the famous rock. The crowd was beginning to disperse since Tomoyose had defeated all challengers. Intent upon not losing any of the spectators, Itosu quickly strode up to the rock and slapped it defiantly. This was all that was needed to bring the crowd back, and within an instant, a huge individual had stepped out to meet Itosu.

He threw a blow, but before it was half way to its target, Itosu had connected with three blows to his head. The man's knees buckled, and he fell to the earth, completely unconscious. It was not long before two irate friends of the defeated man entered the ring with cudgels, cursing Itosu and his town. They circled to either side of Itosu and, with a given signal, attacked him simultaneously. Without waiting for them to converge upon him, Itosu lunged to the right. blocking the downward arc of the man's swing at his forearm with both hands. A mere split second after this, Itosu leaned his upper body downward and thrust his back foot out in a side kick which caught the second man squarely on the chin and knocked his feet out from under him. Still holding the first man by his weapon arm, Itosu now planted his rear leg and kicked upward into the man's groin with the instep of his other foot. Three men now lay within the boundaries of the makeshift arena, two of them lying peacefully, and the other writhing breathlessly on the ground.

"Is there no man left with the nerve to meet a karateka from Shuri?" asked Itosu after looking around him slowly.

"Player of parlor games," bellowed a deep and powerful voice, "I consider myself challenged."

An enormous man, brawnier than Itosu himself, emerged arrogantly from the crowd Itosu's eyes

. . . . Itosu quickly strode up to the rock and slapped it defiantly.

flickered for an instant with surprise, recognizing Tomoyose, and he grimly thought he would have to dispose of this man quickly; if he didn't, the advantage of strength would quickly go over to his opponent.

The two men stepped up, put their arms on the rock *ude-kake-shi*, and warily circled each other. The crowd was laying bets, the odds ten to one against the man from Shuri. Tomoyose suddenly lunged in with a blow mighty enough to fell an ox. Itosu blocked, chopped Tomoyose across the arm with a shuto and jumped to the side. The crowd heard a snap, like a dry twig breaking, when Itosu delivered his shuto across Tomoyose's arm. They looked at their hero, who was grimacing with pain, his arm dangling broken at his side. The great Tomoyose had been defeated by a man from Shuri.

Tomoyose suddenly lunged in with a blow mighty enough to fell an ox.

Following this, Itosu's name spread throughout Naha. He became the man to beat if one were going to make a name for oneself. It was not long after this confrontation that Itosu received yet another test. He had been on his way home when he passed a tavern and heard his name called out from inside the door. He turned to see an old acquaintance, who greeted him warmly and persuaded him to come into the tavern for a few rounds of drinks and affable conversation. While they passed the time, the sun set so that it was quite dark when Itosu finally resumed his journey. It was a cloudy night with a full moon intermittantly illuminating the Daido pine forest. As so often occurred in those lawless times, he was suddenly set upon by bandits.

"If his purse is as fat as his head, he will be a fine catch," said the first bandit in a rasping voice to the other two.

Itosu looked at the speaker and noticed he carried a sai. Another held a six-foot bo in his hands while the third was weaponless. At this time, the words of his teacher, Matsumura, came back to him. "If you should ever find yourself facing a multiple attack, you must first dispose of the weapon that can be thrown before concentrating on the other weapons."

As the moon passed behind a thick cloud, Itosu grabbed his opportunity right in the middle of the first man's sentence. He jumped upward, grabbed a branch above him, and swung himself up into the tree and out of sight. The man with the sai cocked his arm to throw it, but wisely decided to keep a hold of it instead. It changed nothing, for, as he began to look for a better vantage point from which to spot Itosu, the would-be victim of robbery jumped down upon him, knocking him to the ground. Itosu wrung the sai from his hands and quickly broke the bandits's neck with a shuto.

The man with the bo was next, running too late to aid his friend. After only a few seconds of sparring with this man, Itosu became convinced that he was no mere novice with the weapon. To keep pace, Itosu backpedaled furiously with the sai held over his head. He suddenly realized that the man was using a great many motions from a bo kata known as *shiu shi no kon*.[5] Itosu, knowing he was taking a tremendous gamble, decided to anticipate a feint with the bo, which was customarily used in the kata. At the proper moment, he flung the sai with a snap of his wrists.

He had guessed correctly. As the second bandit feinted in with the bo, the sai imbedded itself deep into his chest. His death was instantaneous.

Upon seeing this, the weaponless man broke and ran. He lived to spread the incredible tale of Itosu's fighting prowess, which contributed to the man's already ponderous reputation.

Yet, in spite of his awesome demeanor, there were always some men who were willing to stake their lives on the chance that he could be beaten. In 1905, when he was 75 years old, these men still came in hopes of walking away with the prize of being the individual who defeated the old master. But he had lost none of his prowess to the sands of time. What he had lost in physical ability, he seemed to make up in sheer power of the will.

> The man with the sai cocked his arm to throw it .

At this time, Okinawa had slipped completely under the domination of Japan. It was a Japan which was just beginning to flex its muscles before the world, shocking even its own optimists with a decisive victory over the Russian navy at Port Arthur. Yet, even while its steel ships had run amock through those of a nation nearly 300 times its size, its dominion of Okinawa was still locked into perfection of the martial arts.

One day during this period, a Naichi[6] policeman issued a challenge to the local karateka, belittling their art. Itosu, who was presently responsible for shaping the physical education curriculum in the Okinawan high schools, felt stung when he heard the comment and, much like he had so many years before, decided to do something about it.

He was troubled, however, and went to the high school principal.

"Soon you will see karate in a true fighting situation . . . . "

"Karate is not a sport," said Itosu, "but rather, a killing art. It should only be used for self-defense and as a last resort."

The principal, who regarded Itosu very highly, agreed and went to the Kencho for further advice. The prefectural officials who made up this council were all Japanese from the mainland near Kagoshima. They were from the same town as the boisterous policeman who had caused all the commotion, and they regarded him as invincible.

"I think this would be a good opportunity for us to see how karate compares to the art of judo," said one of the officials. "It is already my considered opinion that the match should be allowed to take place. Only then will you Okinawans realize that the Naichi art is far superior to your karate."

When Itosu heard that the match had been officially allowed, he gathered all of his students and instructed them soberly. "Soon you will see karate in a true fighting situation, for I have decided to meet the judo expert myself. I will not kill him, of course, but I must convince the mainlanders that karate is the most fearful of all of the empty-hand arts. This is why I want all of you to see the match."

The confrontation of the two great martial arts, judo vs. karate, was set to take place in mid-afternoon, and the school grounds were overflowing with spectators hours before, most of whom were Japanese mainlanders who took little trouble to conceal their disdain for karate. A sudden silence fell upon the hecklers when the 75-year-old man entered the arena on behalf of karate.

Then the crowd's unrest grew to indignation. They were outraged at what seemed to be an insult to their judo expert. His victory would lose all of its meaning if he merely beat an old man, they thought. For this reason, the fight was almost postponed, and indeed, would have been if it weren't for 75-year-old Itosu's tremendous reputation. It was with reservations, however, that the judo expert entered the ring.

He circled Itosu, half-clowning in order to save some face, while the old man calmly pivoted and kept his eyes on him. Itosu was so completely relaxed that he looked somewhat ridiculous—even to his own students. Suddenly, the policeman lunged forward and grasped Itosu by his sleeve and collar, but in a flicker, the crowd was astonished to see the policeman slump to the ground. Itosu had driven his left fist deep into the young man's solar plexus, accompanied by a loud but curt kiai. The young man lay gasping for breath at his feet.

It was so sudden, the Japanese officials were speechless. They only heard a single kiai, and suddenly, their vaunted champion was down. Itosu calmly bent over, applied a *katsu* with his aged and liver-spotted hands, and the fallen opponent sat up, stunned but revived.

Itosu turned to the gallery where his students sat and spoke to them in his crackling voice, which was plainly heard amidst the stunned silence of the crowd.

"Today," he said, "you have seen what karate can do against the uninitiated. Never should one use it unless there is no other recourse. Let today's match

A sudden silence fell upon the hecklers when the 75-year-old man entered the arena .

be the lesson you will always remember."

In so saying, he sauntered out of sight and into history.

Today, Itosu is remembered mainly through his kata. His concentration during his teaching years centered around fulfillment of each person's individual physique. He realized that each person had to develop his body to the highest possible perfection, for himself and for his purpose. To put the body under complete control of the mind was necessary before any other type of development could take place. Itosu knew the kata was best for this.

He felt the mobilization of the body, control of the breath, stilling of the mind and concentration are made possible through the kata. Itosu believed that through karate, man can channel aggression and rediscover his body as a tool of expression. He epitomized the adage: "A sound mind in a sound body."

He realized that each person had to develop his body to the highest possible perfection . . .

Karate, as practiced today, owes much to Itosu. He used the kata not only for physical self-defense, but also as a means of characterological transformation. He said: "Karate is a way of life, a means to achieve complete security and fearlessness."

To him, karate was a matter of character and not a means to a fight, or to glory.

NOTES FOR ITOSU YASUTSUNE

1. Meijin: one who has mastered his art far beyond the boundaries of physical prowess. One becomes a meijin only after experiencing infinitely painstaking discipline.

2. The Japanese took King Sho-Iku and other Okinawan members of the nobility to Tokyo and practically held them in bondage to insure their control over the Okinawan islands. This political practice was fairly common during the Tokugawa Shogunate and was continued by Japan until its defeat in World War II.

3. As karate grew in popularity through the public school physical education program, an intense rivalry grew between the cities of Naha and Shuri, characterized by the two major prevailing forms, Sho-Rin and Go-Ju.

4. Ude-kake-shi: a challenge area, most often in the red-light districts where police were apt to look the other way while fights were fought during this pre-jiyukumite (pre-free-fighting) era. Many reputations were made and broken in these rough and tumble confrontations. Itosu withstood a number of attacks, both single and multiple, from fellow Okinawans and even sailors from the Western countries. He bore many scars from these encounters but never once lost a fight.

5. Shiu Shi no kon: a bo kata, brought to Okinawa by a Chinese martial artist.

6. Naichi: a term used by the mainland Japanese to distinguish themselves from the Okinawans. Literally translated, the word means interior, inland or home.

Kyan Chotoku

A NOTHER OF BUSHI MATSUMURA'S ILLUS-
TRIOUS STUDENTS WAS KYAN CHOTOKU, a
martial artist who believed that order is heaven's
first law. Born in Shuri, Okinawa, he went into the
martial arts at the tender age of eight. Only a child,
the discipline required made a lifelong impression on
him. He emerged with a sense of order and justice
beyond the comprehension of most men.[1]

He lived in Shuri until the age of 30 and then
spent the rest of his life in Katena where he taught at
a karate dojo near Hisabashi. Slim to the point of
being skinny, it is said he was master of the jump.
Among the masters in Okinawan history, Kyan was
without a peer when it came to kicking techniques.
His double jump kick was without an equal.

However, in spite of his proficiency in foot
techniques, he was a total martial artist and never
considered himself a specialist. Once it came to his
ears that his students, proud of his skill, had entered
into hot debate with others claiming that though the
hand is faster, the foot is stronger. They imputed that
Kyan was the strongest karate master around.

Kyan put the controversy to rest with swift
dispatch. He said, "One should use both for optimum
results. Relying too heavily on one or the other will
cause an imbalance in self-defense. It can be said that
the hands are like the infantry, and the feet like the

artillery. Without the protection of the infantry, the batteries are helpless, and without the support of the artillery, the infantry will sustain many casualties."

Kyan practiced the seisan[2] for two years and perfected the kata. The incessant drill and pedantic attention to detail required for mastery of a kata made a profound impression on him. He developed a philosophy of respect for the law, and he believed that only the undisciplined would easily break the law.

In his time, the main street leading to Naha from Shuri was under the control of a group of hooligans. The hooligans managed to gain control by routing the police, who tried to arrest them for crimes such as mugging, rape and other physical acts of violence.

He developed a philosophy of respect for the law . . . .

The gang stationed themselves on a hill situated halfway on the road leading from Shuri to Naha and demanded toll for safe passage between the two cities. In time, traffic came to a complete halt before twilight and barely inched along during noon hour. Only large groups traveled together for protection. Woe to the lonely traveller caught on the road after sundown.

The matter became so bad that the townspeople in Shuri held a meeting and came to a unanimous decision that only the great Kyan could solve the problem. The police were so afraid, they did not venture out of the town limits at night.

Kyan had just finished training when the townspeople called on him. The spokesman for the group explained the situation.

"Sensei, you are our last hope. The hērē[3] is getting out of hand."

"Why don't you good people go to the police?" asked Kyan. "They are the minions of the law."

"Sensei, if the police could do something, we would have put the matter in their hands. But they were routed by the here and will not venture out of the city."

Kyan was surprised at this information and listened to all that had transpired prior to the meeting of the people. He then agreed.

Every night for a week, Kyan carried two chickens, one under each arm and, singing loudly, passed the hill at night. Nothing happened.

Then on a clear moonlit night as Kyan passed the hill, four young men jumped out from the side of the road and accosted him.

"Hey skinny! Where did you come from and where are you going?" One of them taunted.

"On my way home to Shuri. I have just come from Naha with two chickens that I have purchased. My mother is sick, and we need the chickens for broth," Kyan tried to keep walking, but three of the men blocked his way.

"Money or your life," they demanded.

Kyan laughed. "I have some small change left after the purchase of the chickens, and I am not about to give any money to you or anyone else for that matter."

. . . . he jabbed his hands against the two men directly in front of him .

"We are not playing games," growled the leader in front.

"Okay, if you want my small change so badly, you can have it." And Kyan parted with his money and made ready to leave.

"Hold on, we are not finished with you. Give us the chickens."

One of the hooligans held his sword in front of him in a threatening gesture.

Kyan looked at the hooligan intently and said, "Well, it looks like money and chickens measured against human life is not much. Okay, if you want the chickens so badly, take them. Here!" And he flung both chickens at the men in front of him.

At the instant he flung the chickens, he jabbed his hands against the two men directly in front of him, poking one in the eye and the other in the throat. Both dropped on the spot. He quickly kicked the sword bearer in the groin and turned to face the hooligan in the back of him.

The action happened so fast that when Kyan turned, the hooligan that was standing in the back of him just drew a sharp breath. He looked at Kyan's face and lost his nerve. As Kyan advanced, the tough broke and ran.

Kyan then turned to the three toughs sprawled on the ground and said, "I am ready. Next time we meet it will be to the death. Today was just a lesson in manners. You have tried to destroy the fabric of society and you have tried to make lawlessness pay. Strict adherence to law and order makes life orderly and bearable. There is no reason to make it tougher for the poor."

The people of Shuri, when recounting this story, relate how Kyan passed the street every night for the next fortnight. The street had become safe for travel again.

"Next time we meet, it will be to the death."

If one should ever visit Katena and look at the area where Kyan had operated his dojo, one would see that it was near Hisabashi bridge. According to stories handed down, Kyan practiced jumping from a barge anchored below the bridge and was able to jump backward up and over onto the bridge. He did this while practicing the kata seisan.

He also had an unbendable arm such as current day aikido practitioners sometimes use to demonstrate the wonders of *ki*. When Kyan was an old man, he would demonstrate at public festivals and special school occasions. Young and old alike would go up to him and try to bend his arm, which he held extended in front of him. Their efforts were to no avail. No one, as far as historians know, had ever been successful in bending his arm.[4]

He was such a thin, old man that most people were perplexed by the question, "What is the secret of your skill and strength? Men three times younger than you cannot move you at all. What is it?"

The answer was always the same: "Develop your *tanden*. Drop your mind there and operate all your actions from there. Practice your kata until your kata moves from your tanden. When you *become* the kata, you have achieved the secret."

KYAN CHOTOKU

NOTES FOR KYAN CHOTOKU

1."Bushi" Matsumura, Kyan Chotoku's sensei, recognized the unusual qualities in his young student and imposed the type of training that would have done justice to a Zen temple. Kyan, nicknamed "Migwha" (due to his eyes), believed self-discipline and stability in society went hand-in-hand.

2.The seisan was the first kata taught by the Okinawan masters prior to 1903, when Itosu Yasutsune taught in the public school system. Since then, karate schools have taught the pinan kata, or introductory kata, before going into the classical ones. Some masters still cling to the tradition and teach the seisan first. One notable example of this is the Shimabukuro brothers, Eizo and Tatsuo, both of whom studied under Kyan.

3.Here: a hooligan (Okinawan dialect). Also, a ruffian or a tough. In that era, as the story indicates, martial artists were often called upon to deal with these here.

4.Kyan was said to have such complete control of his ki that he could root himself to the ground by extending it down through his legs and into the ground by about a foot.

Yabu Kentsu

IN OKINAWA AROUND 1903, karate was incorporated into the public school physical education programs. A prime mover in this innovation was Nishimura Mitsuya, the president of Shihan-Gakko (teacher's college). It was Mitsuya's vision that karate training would build moral strength in teachers and students alike. To implement the program, Mitsuya called upon Itosu Yasutsune and his top student, Yabu Kentsu.[1]

Prior to this period, karate training was restricted to the nobility and men of means. Due to Itosu's organizational ability, the high schools in Okinawa gradually accepted the new karate program.

Itosu went once a week to Shihan-Gakko, where Yabu Kentsu, affectionately known as "The Sergeant," taught daily.[2] Yabu was a graduate of Kashi-Yoseisho (a non-commissioned officers' school) and a stickler for basics. As a youth, he had always been very powerful and quickly rose to the top directly under Itosu. He was known for his extreme strength and excellent techniques. During the Sino-Japanese War, he fought on the Chinese mainland with the Japanese Expeditionary Forces and attained the rank of lieutenant—quite an accomplishment in those days.[3]

On the battlefield while fighting against the Chinese forces, Yabu perfected his karate and developed a style that was deadly and effective. When he returned to Okinawa as a lieutenant in the Japanese Army after the war, people called him "The Sergeant," a name that stuck with him to his dying day. As his fame grew, people started asking, "What kind of martial artist is this Sergeant?"

At this time, another star was rising on the karate horizon—Choki Motobu.[4] Motobu was born of nobility, free from the rigors of earning his own living, so he spent all of his time training in karate. As his fame grew, people began to consider him Yabu's equal, and the obvious question arose as to which of the two was superior.

Eventually, a *shiai* (match) was arranged at the Motobu Goten (Motobu palace). Choki Motobu had his servants clear a large reception room in the palace, making it bare of even the *tatami* (floor mats), so the contestants could fight on the floor. No one was allowed in the room except the chosen newspaper correspondents and a few close friends.

Yabu and Motobu faced each other. The air crackled with the sound of loud kiais, shuffling feet, punches and kicks slapping human flesh, and the excited gasps of the few privileged viewers. The spectators were witnessing a fight the likes of which was probably never to be seen again.

> The spectators were witnessing a fight, the likes of which was never to be seen again.

After 20 minutes, Yabu's great wartime experience and his deadly karate, forged on the battlefield, gave him an edge. Motobu was defeated for the first and only time in his illustrious career. Both men had trained arduously for this shiai, and there were no serious injuries, although both were badly bruised. They parted as good friends—determined to improve Okinawan karate.

*   *   *   *

It is to Yabu's credit that he did not seriously injure anyone in his lifetime, except in war. Once he made a journey to Yonabaru and left Naha around dusk. While walking around Tsubokawa, five men sprang out from the roadside and blocked the street. Yabu tried to detour around them, but they blocked his every move. When he stopped, they suddenly attacked him. Not wanting to harm the hooligans but determined to resume his journey, Yabu threw one man into a clump of bushes and tossed another at his companions. The rest fled.

* * * *

Yabu Kentsu produced many karate greats in his lifetime. Nakaima, Kyan, Taira, Toyama, Sakihana, Motoda, and Shiroma are just a few. Around 1927, he made a trip to Los Angeles to see his son, and on his return trip to Okinawa, Kentsu stopped over in Hawaii for several months to teach and give lectures.

Since the Sergeant had forged his deadly karate on the battlefield, he truly could not accept karate as a sport.

"Karate is a way of life," he once said, "It builds character unlike that which is built through sport. One does not practice karate for fun or for a prize."

During his lifetime, Yabu Kentsu lived by these words.

. . . . .Yabu threw one man into a clump of bushes and tossed another at his companions.

NOTES FOR YABU KENTSU

1.Yabu was not a student of Itosu Yasutsune in the sense that he studied in Itosu's dojo. Both studied under Matsumura. Itosu, however, was the senior student and Yabu took most of his lessons with Itosu in charge. In this sense, we can say that Itosu was his teacher.

2.Yabu taught under the supervision of Itosu, who was responsible for karate education in the public schools.

3.The Naichi, or mainland Japanese, subtly discriminated against the Okinawans, whom they felt were not "true" Japanese. Thus, Yabu's promotion in the Japanese Army is testament to how great his achievements were.

4.Choki Motobu: a karate great and legendary figure. He is historically linked to the creation of the Kempo karate schools which originated in the Hawaiian islands.

Itoman Bunkichi

ITOMAN IS A PROVINCE ON THE SOUTHERN TIP OF OKINAWA. During the feudal era of Japan when Europeans were discouraged from entering Japan, Okinawa was the natural stopping place for foreign ships trying to gain entry to Japan. Some succeeded, and some did not.

The Okinawans were friendly and permitted ships to lay over for as long as they wanted. Being a suzerain of China, it was natural that ships from China and Korea plied a regular trade, making frequent short trips to Okinawa. For the European ships, however, it was a different matter. Europe was a long three months or so away, and ships from that part of the world laid over for long periods of time in Okinawa without the regular itinerary that the Oriental ships had.

The majority of European traders at that time were Dutch and Portuguese, therefore ships from those countries composed the major portion of foreign ships that anchored at the Okinawan ports. It was only a matter of time before the European sailors, far and long removed from their native lands, consorted with the Okinawan women.

Although the majority of the sailors fulfilled their needs in the red light districts of Naha, there were some who crossed the racial line and married Okinawan women. Most of the Dutch sailors who intermarried chose their wives from the widows of Itoman, a fisherman's province where many young Okinawan males were lost to the ravages of typhoons and heavy seas. The Europeans did not mind the ready-made families that the Okinawan bachelors shied away from.

These marriages produced Eurasian offspring, known to the Japanese as *ainoko* (halfbreeds). Prior to the Pacific War and the subsequent occupation of Japan by Westerners, any fair-skinned, light-eyed halfbreed Okinawan was almost always found to be from the province of Itoman. Itoman Bunkichi was one of them.

Because he was a halfbreed, the name of Itoman Bunkichi was forever excluded from the pages of Okinawan karate history. The combination of the Tanaka Manifesto in the Twenties, the emergence of the Japanese military clique in the Thirties, and the confrontation with the United States and the resultant Pacific War of the Forties added to the already existing social opprobrium of anyone not of 100-percent pure Japanese heritage. Ainokos were expunged and deleted from all written records, especially in the martial arts.

... he was filled with anger and resentment aimed at the native population.

Be that as it may, Itoman Bunkichi's place in history as one of Okinawa's greatest martial artists is not to be denied. Bunkichi reached great heights of physical perfection and technique. He was without an equal in acrobatic manuevers.

One summer day during the Japanese Restoration,[1] a samurai was walking alongside a river. This samurai was not schooled in the proper conduct befitting one of his class, and he was filled with anger and resentment aimed at the native population, whom he considered beneath his station in life. He was in this warped state of mind when he encountered a huge Okinawan in conversation with a girl, laughing and talking at the junction of a road and a bridge. Spoiling for a fight, the samurai had found a target for his resentment in the huge Okinawan. The Japanese swaggered up to the Okinawan and suddenly lurched towards him, but he fell against empty air for the Okinawan had shifted his body just enough to get out of the way. He stood there talking to the girl as though the samurai was not even there.

Infuriated, the samurai deliberately charged again in another attempt to knock down the Okinawan. Again, the Okinawan side-stepped. The girl, anxious of the impressively dressed Japanese, tugged at her companion's sleeve and motioned for them to get away.

The samurai was filled with anger now because he felt he had "lost face" to a lowly Okinawan native. He drew out his *katana* (sword) and yelled out, "Oi, ainoko!² Trying to make a fool of me, eh? Fight like a man instead of slipping away!"

The Okinawan turned to face him, and the samurai was startled by the hazel color of his eyes. "I'm going to teach you a lesson," the samurai said, "and make an example of you." He charged with his drawn blade.

Bunkichi ran to the rail of the bridge and jumped over it. The samurai stopped his charge and peered over the rail to see if the Okinawan had hit the water. No splash was heard. The samurai leaned farther over the rail to see what had happened when he was suddenly pushed from behind and toppled into the water.

When Bunkichi had jumped over the rail, he had grabbed the support rail below, swung over to the other side like a monkey swinging in the trees and catapulted himself onto the opposite side of the bridge. It was a feat that only a monkey or ape could have been able to perform, but to Itoman Bunkichi, it was child's play.

*   *   *   *

As the years passed and his legend grew, Bunkichi was credited with jumping over the rail and coming up on the other side without the use of his hands. Even today some people in Hawaii will swear that Itoman Bunkichi could indeed jump over a bridge,

Infuriated, the samurai deliberately charged again . . . .

soar like a bird and come up on the other side in one loop.[3]

*   *   *   *

Since Itoman Bunkichi was exceptionally huge and strong by Okinawan standards, he developed considerable skill in subduing would-be strong men without resorting to strikes or hits of any kind. Instead, he pushed, repelled, or nullified would-be attackers in the manner of a ju-jutsu or aikido expert. He was afraid of killing a person with a blow because of his awesome power.

Once when he was walking alongside a stone wall, two persons attacked him, and he responded by jumping over the wall, disappearing from sight. It was reported by those who saw the incident that "one minute he was there, and the next minute he was gone."

" . . . . if you duplicate my feat, I will accept your challenge."

After Itoman Bunkichi's affair with the samurai became known (thanks to the girl who was with him at the time), many martial artists came to Itoman to challenge him. He skillfully made short work of them without raising a hand. He simply agreed to a match only if they could duplicate his feat. He would say, "You have come to challenge me because of my feat. Well, if you duplicate my feat, I shall accept your challenge." No one succeeded. There were several that managed to catch the support rail with one hand and swing over to the other side with the other hand, but no one managed to swing himself up and onto the bridge.

"He must be half-ape," most of them muttered as they went away. And many were secretly pleased they had failed after seeing Bunkichi in the flesh with his awesome hands and shoulders.

*   *   *   *

However, there are always the skeptical and the foolish. One such person was named "Kame." He was named after the turtle, considered wise and long-living. Unlike the turtle, he was not wise, and the only reason he was living after an encounter with

Itoman Bunkichi was due to Bunkichi's hesitance to harm anyone.

Kame, born a commoner like Itoman Bunkichi, secretly resented the martial artists in Okinawa who had position not only because of their skill but also because of their inherent birthright. Born a commoner, Kame could never become a samurai, and this shut off all prospects of ever becoming a teacher with a dojo.

He was pleasantly surprised when the exploits of Itoman Bunkichi reached his ears. He heard that Itoman Bunkichi was a commoner, yet because of his skills, was sought after as a teacher and was respected even by the upper class. The idea of defeating Itoman Bunkichi intrigued him and, in time, became an obsession. As time went by, Kame became desperate. He, as so many before him, went to Bunkichi and challenged him. He could not pass the bridge test imposed by Bunkichi as prerequisite to a match.

Stubbornly, Kame stayed near. He inquired about the habits of Bunkichi and followed him like a shadow. But there was always someone around, and he could not make his move for fear of ridicule. Too many had seen him fail the test.

After many days without the prospect of ever finding Bunkichi alone, Kame was beginning to ger dejected and wondered if fame was worth the chase. He was walking by a village when Bunkichi, deep in thought, cut in front of him a little way down the path. Elated, Kame charged Bunkichi and threw a tremendous punch. Bunkichi turned and pushed the Turtle to one side, sending him flying headlong into a clump of bushes.

Kame recovered and charged again. Bunkichi simply spun, avoided Kame's rush and continued his walk. Kame was furious and shouted, "Stand up and fight like a man."

Bunkichi simply smiled.

This infuriated Kame as he saw visions of his own splendor vanishing. Frothing at the mouth, he charged headlong toward Bunkichi, who was standing

> The idea of defeating Itoman Bunkichi intrigued him .

next to a house. As Kame charged, Itoman Bunkichi leapt upward, grabbed the eaves of the nearby roof and swung himself completely over to the other side of the house. From there, he walked away while Kame, on the other side of the house, slammed into the wall and sank to the earth, stunned and unconscious. Fortunately for Kame, he had a head like stone. The only serious injuries he received were the blow to his pride and a bump on his head. He realized that Bunkichi had spared him great injury. Chastised, he went back home to raising his pigs.

* * * *

Another tale of Itoman Bunkichi deals with his willingness to aid others in distress and is longer and more detailed than other stories of his exploits.

Bunkichi visited Naha during the height of the shipping season when many ships were in the harbor and the city was filled with activity. He strolled among the seamen going in and out of the many inns and bars in the gay quarters of Naha. He was stopped by loud shouts emanating from a side street. Curious, he approached the direction of the furor and saw a large crowd gathering around what appeared to be a group of seamen rousting an Okinawan.

He peered over the heads of the mob and saw an old man being harassed by a Portuguese seaman, a huge, bearded giant with earrings. Another person was pleading with the giant on behalf of the old man, who refused to speak for himself. The giant seemed oblivious to the pleadings and continued to shove the old man against the crowd, which kept pushing him back toward the giant. Bunkichi watched for a few minutes then stepped into the center of the commotion. He asked the spokesman, "What is going on? Why is the giant pushing the old man?"

"He is angry because the old man will not give him any credit to buy drinks and girls," the interpreter replied. "He was here about three months ago, ran up a huge bill and promised to pay the next time he was in Naha. He still has not paid, and now he wants more credit. The old man refused and caused his anger."

He was stopped by loud shouts emanating from a side street.

"Tell him," Bunkichi said, pointing to the giant, "that he is not welcome here, and it would be wise if he and his shipmates went back on board ship without causing any more trouble."

During this time, the seamen were growing restless, amazed at the rash imposition of this Okinawan. When the interpreter related Bunkichi's message, the Portuguese grew even angrier, spurred on by the sudden burst of laughter from his shipmates.

The Portuguese giant grabbed for Itoman Bunkichi's arm with the intention of pushing him towards the crowd as he had done with the old man when, to his surprise, Bunkichi easily eluded his grasp, starring into his eyes. Startled by the hazel color of his eyes, the giant mistook Bunkichi for a European and shouted, "What are you doing in Okinawan clothes? How dare you stop our fun. You should be with us instead of against us."

The crowd began to stir restlessly, sensing an impending fight.

Bunkichi calmly listened to the interpreter and repeated what he had said before, "Tell them to go back to their ship peacefully." His anger, usually so well-guarded, was beginning to show.

Someone stepped out from the crowd, held his hands up for quiet, and said, "I am the ship's master. Why don't you and Pereira here have it out. Winner take all. If Pereira loses, he pays all his bills and damages. If you lose, Pereira owes nothing and all is square."

"Agreed," Bunkichi answered and turned to face Pereira. The giant seaman looked at his cronies and smiled in anticipation. He winked at the girls who were watching from the doorways, rubbed his hands, and charged at Bunkichi with his arms flailing like windmills. Pereira was known as the terror of Lorenco Marques.[4] His reputation was so legendary that when children cried in the African villages, mothers used to quiet them by saying, "Shh. Don't cry or Pereira will hear you and come." It is said that he left many broken bones between Lisbon and

During this time, the seamen were growing restless .

Macao. He would sooner fight than eat.

As Pereira charged, Bunkichi slapped Pereira's left arm at the elbow and pushed him headlong into the crowd. The crowd pushed Pereira back and he snarled. His eyes gleamed and he circled Bunkichi, who just stood and watched.

Then Pereira jabbed with his left, and Bunkichi stepped out of range. Pereira feinted with his right, but Bunkichi did not move. He knew a feint when he saw one, and he knew that Pereira was trying to set him up. Pereira shuffled in fast and threw a combination punch. Again, Bunkichi stepped out of range.

Pereira stopped, put his hands down, and beckoned to Bunkichi to fight, winking at the crowd at the same time. The crowd laughed and guffawed with approval. Bets began to change hands. The betting was not a matter of who was going to win. It was a foregone conclusion as far as the seamen were concerned; it was only a matter of time before Pereira would finish off the Okinawan. No one gave Bunkichi a chance.

Bunkichi quickly stepped out of range and kicked Pereira sharply on the right wrist.

As Pereira beckoned with his hands, Bunkichi just waited and smiled. All the seamen started yelling, "Come on, you yellow bastard. Fight, damn it. Fight." But still, Bunkichi did not move.

Then Pereira lost his patience, charged and threw a barrage of punches. Bunkichi stepped quickly out of range and kicked Pereira sharply on the right wrist. Pereira dropped his right hand and glared at the Okinawan upstart. Bunkichi's kick was hard enough to numb the arm all the way to the elbow, but the veteran Portuguese fighter did not appear to be affected by the blow. But he realized that he was up against something he had never seen before. He quickly changed from clowning to serious fighting. He began to maneuver Bunkichi into range, trying to corner him so that he could no longer elude his blows. He shuffled, feinted, and moved into preparation for his favorite blow, the Danish Kiss,[5] but Bunkichi was too quick and slipped away. The circle began to tighten as the anxious watchers closed in. Pereira smiled as he noticed this, believing the smaller space would limit Bunkichi's defenses. Bunkichi stopped for a moment and the Portuguese leapt at him, grabbing him in his arms. "At last!" Pereira thought, and smashed his head toward Bunkichi's nose. This was Pereira's famous coup de grace.

A sailor shouted out, "This is it! In Singapore, Pereira finished off the Hindu wrestling champion with the Danish Kiss."

The group gasped as Bunkichi seemed to fall to one side, but there was no sound of breaking bone. Then suddenly, Pereira was flying through the air. Bunkichi had executed a *yoko-sutemi* at the instant that Pereira grabbed him. The timing was so perfect that even the Portuguese thought that he had broken Bunkichi's nose. When he landed, Bunkichi jumped on top of him, slamming an elbow strike to his temple. The Portuguese lay unconscious, and the seamen were stunned.

The captain stepped forward and said to Bunkichi, "If I had not witnessed this myself, I would not have thought it possible. I do not know how you did whatever you did, but as far as I am concerned, it was magic." He pointed to Pereira and asked, "Is he dead?"

Bunkichi kneeled down and applied a *katsu*.[6] Finally, Pereira opened his eyes and asked, "What happened?" He got up, ready to fight again when he saw Bunkichi, but the captain intervened. "Enough. You were beaten by a wizard. Come on, let's go back to the ship." One by one, all the men dispersed.

The news of Bunkichi's victory spread through the town like wildfire. People converged on the spot where the fight had taken place. Above all, they wanted to meet Bunkichi.

Itoman Bunkichi had disappeared as if with the wind. He had left as quietly as he had come.

History is vague as to where he went, and even vaguer when it comes to his method of training and who his instructor was.

> The group gasped as Bunkichi seemed to fall to one side . . . .

THE WEAPONLESS WARRIORS

The stories of Itoman Bunkichi are handed down through the generations by word of mouth. Needless to say, some of the stories about him would stretch the imaginations of most people, but truth is sometimes stranger than fiction, and the fact remains that Itoman Bunkichi did exist. The bridge that made him famous still stands in Okinawa, and his exploits remain in the hearts of those who heard his tales at the knees of their elders.

NOTES FOR ITOMAN BUNKICHI

The bridge that made him famous still stands in Okinawa . . . .

1. Meiji era: a reign which started in 1866. The so-called "Restoration" began several years prior to the establishment of Emperor Meiji on the throne, after the overthrow of the Tokugawa Shogunate (1603-1867).

2. The last few years of the Tokugawa Shogunate produced one of the most bitter civil wars in Japanese history. The samurai remaining loyal to the Shogunate passionately hated anything which smacked of the European world. They called all Europeans "hairy foreigners," and considered half-breeds as belonging to the lowest social order. This view is no longer valid in modern Japan. In fact, one might say just the opposite is so. To be half-white is now considered fortunate and superior. Japanese men are especially enamored of white women and Eurasians travel in the best circles.

3. The Okinawan community in Hawaii and Brazil still remember Itoman Bunkichi. When inquiries were made about him in post-war Okinawa, however, he was only vaguely recalled. This is not surprising since the Okinawan people who settled in Hawaii around the turn of the century were sure to keep the oral tradition alive in spite of the rise of Japanese militarism.

4. Lorenco Marques: a town in Portuguese East Africa. Prior to World War II, when the author visited Macao, the legend of Pereira, the terror of Lorenco Marques, was still alive. The Portuguese version is that this man was beaten by a Japanese samurai, but only after he had dispatched several of them. This version loses its credibility in light of the fact that samurai would have used their swords and would never have engaged in a brawl in the red light district.

5. Danish Kiss: a common fighting practice spread by many of the tough European sailors. It involved grabbing the opponent by the lapels with both hands and butting him squarely on the nose with one's head.

6. Katsu: a technique of revival used on fallen or injured men who have been rendered unconscious. Most karate practitioners are skillful in katsu.

Matsumora Kosaku

BEFORE THE ADVENT OF FREE-FIGHTING (jiyukumite) in Okinawa, the contest grounds for testing karate skills were in the port city of Naha, in and around the red light district called Naha-tsuji-machi. Many legendary fights took place there.

In one period after Okinawa became a prefectural part of Japan, a strong-arm braggart was always instigating and winning fights in this area. He bellowed, roared and blustered around the district, beating up seamen from foreign ships, making life miserable for visitors in the area.

One day, he picked on a rickshaw driver. The little man threw him into the waters of the harbor with ease, and thenceforth dampened the braggart's ardor for hand-to-hand combat.

This incident was written up in the *Asahi Shimbun* by columnist Sugiyama Heisuke, who followed up the story with keen observation or rickshaw men working in the dock area.

At that time, according to this particular observation, visitors arriving at Naha Harbor were greeted with the sight of rickshaw men with noble mien, waiting for their customers. Most of these rickshaw men were from Tomari-machi, two kilometers from Naha-Shi. They were from the bushi (samurai) class, which had fallen into hard times, forcing them into the rickshaw trade to earn enough to eat. Most of them worked in the evenings when the gay quarters opened and continued until the wee hours of the morning.

The newspaper article focused attention to the fact that these men were or had been students of Matsumora Kosaku, a karate master who lived in Tomari and taught a style that was passed down from the "Birdman." Makabe Chokun was one of Sakugawa's disciples.

The braggart had been thrown into the waters of the harbor by one of these men. As a result, *Tomari-Te* gained the attention it so richly deserved, and Matsumora Kosaku became known to the general populace.

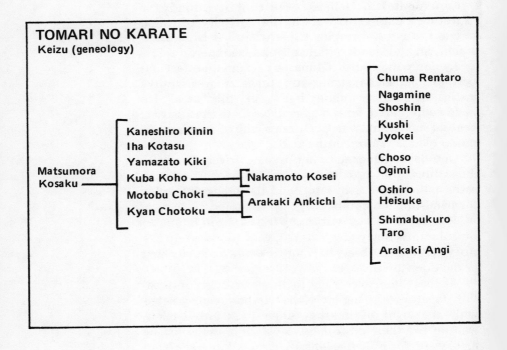

TOMARI NO KARATE
Keizu (geneology)

Matsumora Kosaku

Kaneshiro Kinin
Iha Kotasu
Yamazato Kiki
Kuba Koho ——— Nakamoto Kosei
Motobu Choki
Kyan Chotoku ——— Arakaki Ankichi

Chuma Rentaro
Nagamine Shoshin
Kushi Jyokei
Choso Ogimi
Oshiro Heisuke
Shimabukuro Taro
Arakaki Angi

Choki Motobu

A BIG MAN BY OKINAWAN STANDARDS, Choki Motobu enjoyed all of the privileges accorded to his status as a noble. He was loud and colorful, much in the same enjoyable way as some sports heroes are on the American scene today. He commanded that same kind of reverence from the native Okinawans.

To this date, Motobu's principal distinction is that he remains the only karate master ever to knock out a heavyweight ring champion. The story which led up to this distinction is a curious one.

In the early part of the 1920s, Choki Motobu lived in Osaka, Japan, where he befriended a man named Yamaguchi. The two were inseparable; wherever Motobu went, Yamaguchi was sure to accompany him.

One day, Yamaguchi came across an interesting item in the newspaper. The article described mixed bouts which were being held in Tokyo between boxers and judo masters for public viewing. Yamaguchi told his noble friend, and Motobu became convinced that he would enjoy making the journey to Tokyo for such entertainment.

The two set out, wondering how a judoka would fare against a ring fighter.

" 'This heavyweight fighter has never been beaten

in Europe,' " said Yamaguchi, quoting the article, " 'He is the German champion and, when he feels the time is right, he intends to visit America to take the title there.' "

"Perhaps he won't have his title by the time he gets to America," replied Motobu.

"Oh, he'll have it. He has flattened every judo challenger so far."

"Well, perhaps judo isn't the answer, then," Motobu replied thoughtfully.

They attended the matches almost as soon as they arrived in Tokyo. To their amazement, the boxer dispatched every single judoka who entered the ring with almost methodical disinterest. Motobu intently watched the fighter's footwork, impressed and speechless. He danced around the ring and made fools of the judoka.

At long last, the fighter ran through all of his opponents. He arrogantly walked around the perimeter of the ring with his hands raised high in the air, shouting to the crowd.

"Any more? What's the matter? *Was ist los?* Everyone afraid?"

Yamaguchi turned to Choki as silently as he could, so he would not attract the fighter's attention, and asked, "You are from Okinawa, aren't you? I've heard about karate. Do you believe there is anyone in Okinawa who could equal this man?"

"I would say there are five or six," replied Motobu after a period of thought. "I would say there are at least that many in Okinawa who could beat this man."

Yamaguchi found it impossible to believe that tiny, remote Okinawa could produce a single man to even match this fighter, much less five or six that could beat him. As he was expressing this very view, his companion Choki Motobu jumped to his feet and shouted, "I issue a challenge. I will represent Okinawa and Okinawan karate."

Yamaguchi stared at his friend in amazement, tugging at his sleeve.

To their amazement, the boxer dispatched every single judoka who entered the ring .

"Choki! Sit down! I didn't mean for you to take up the gauntlet!"

Stripping to his waist, Motobu ignored his friend's plea and entered the ring. He faced the champion completely relaxed, simply staring into his opponent's eyes. Before long, the fighter shuffled in and attempted a few jabs, which Motobu easily managed to avoid. Slowly but surely, as he used up his arsenal of punches to no avail, the champion began to realize that he was up against an extraordinary fighter.

The boxer finally became careless and threw a powerful right at Motobu's head, but the wily Okinawan ducked underneath and scooted behind him. It was at this point that Motobu demonstrated why he was called "Saru" (monkey). He had a phenomenal ability to leap onto an opponent's back, like a saru. He jumped high in the air and double-kicked his opponent on the way down. When the boxer dropped, Motobu was quickly upon him and choked him into submission.

The people of Tokyo were forced to take notice of karate. All of the city's papers carried detailed accounts of how the obscure karate master subdued the European champion by knocking him flat on his face and choking him into unconsciousness. Motobu's friend, Yamaguchi, was speechless, for he had not known of the man's karate prowess prior to that moment.

He jumped high in the air and double-kicked his opponent on the way down.

* * * *

A few years later, in 1926, Motobu returned to his native Okinawa and made a point to attend the first bullfight of the new season. He went to Nishibaru-Una-Ha in Shuri, where some friends had reserved a seat for him in the front row.

As the excitement of the bullfight grew, Motobu nervously moved his head from side to side, completely caught up in the action. A spectator sitting directly behind him became irritated by his head movement and could no longer control himself. He hit Motobu on the head with his walking stick. In a flash, Motobu had grabbed the stick from the spectator and returned the favor, striking the attacker back on his head. Motobu later said, "I just tapped him on the head for his insolence." But a light tap from Motobu was a heavy blow to the receiver and the spectator fell unconscious.

After the bullfight, Motobu and his friends were on their way home when a gang of youths accosted them and called out, "Hey, you! Big one! You with the bull's body and the donkey's brain. You and your friends are going to pay for beating up that man."

The gang was about twenty-five strong, but Motobu simply turned to his friends and said, "Leave them to me. Go back home and don't worry. I'll be all right." Before his friends could turn to leave, he flung himself into the center of the gang. Amidst the grunts and screams of pain, the cursing and shouting, was Motobu, flailing indefatigably. His friends ran away with fear—for their own lives as well as his.

Before his friends could turn to leave, he flung himself into the center of the gang.

Motobu was thought of as a brawler before he could be considered a serious karateka. He was in his element when he was street fighting, and this case was certainly no exception. He was laughing and shouting as he dealt out punishment, and soon about six or seven of the gang were writhing on the ground. The remainder of the youths broke and fled, leaving Motobu alone in the street. They had learned a painful lesson.

In the meantime, his friends, ashamed of their behavior, were beginning to worry about the safety of Choki Motobu. An hour had passed and still there was no sign of him. One decided to take action:

"Twenty-five people would be too much for anyone. There is no reason we could have expected the Saru to handle them. We better take a look. He may need medical care."

"Wait," said another. "You know how the Saru is. We'd better check his home first."

With that, they ventured to Motobu castle and, as they approached it, the sound of someone pounding the *maki-wara* (straw and wood punching board) grew louder. They ran into the courtyard, only to see that it was Motobu himself, swinging and pounding. Relieved, they asked him about the incident, and he gave them a colorful account of what had transpired.

The story continues to entertain and impress people today as it did then.

*   *   *   *

Choki Motobu never really propagated a school, although many have laid claim to having been his student because he was so widely traveled and such a character. He was probably the most controversial of all karate masters. There are a number of stories, good and bad, which make him a very contradictory figure. Whether a brawler or a serious karateka, let it be said that Choki Motobu left his mark on the evolution of Okinawan karate.

Agena

IN OKINAWA, THERE IS A SMALL PLACE CALLED GUSHIKAWA VILLAGE. It is off the beaten path and not too well known by karate students of today, but it once was the scene of one of the martial arts' most colorful legends.

There is a certain tree in the village which is still the topic of much discussion among local residents. This tree first became famous around the turn of the century when a villager named Agena made history.

Agena, nicknamed "Tairagwaa" (small calm one), was born in the tiny village in 1870, the first son of an upper-middle class family. As a youth, he became one of the first non-noblemen to take up karate and, though only a commoner, was affectionately referred to as a living *bushi* (samurai warrior).[1]

Despite his slight physical stature, he was obsessed with the thought of becoming a man of the "iron fist" and "steel fingers." He pursued this objective with extreme dedication, eventually developing a fist like Thor's hammer. Unlike most karate masters, Agena never opened a school, but instead continued working exclusively with his own fists and fingers until they were capable of performing the incredible feats for which he is now remembered.[2]

One particular day, so the legend says, Agena visited his friend, Tengan Matsu. Tengan knew Agena had developed his hands to a degree which bordered on the supernatural. Tengan opened a bottle of sake and after a few drinks said, "Agena, I'll make a bet with you. I bet I can rip off the bark of that tree faster than you can. The wager will be five pounds of meat. What do you say?"

"Forget it," replied Agena, smiling. "Drink up. It is a silly bet."

"No, I'm serious," insisted Tengan. "But there is a condition. I use my chisel, and you use your hands. After all, you are the man with the iron fist and steel fingers." Tengan smiled, feeling secure in the knowledge that even Agena would not take up such a bet.

Agena then jumped up and said, "Get ready to buy me five pounds of meat." He ran to the tree, and Tengan followed with his chisel.

Tengan called the village headmaster as referee, and they started. Tengan was thinking, "Agena must be drunk. I wonder why he took up such a bet. How can he beat the chisel?"

Agena repeatedly punched the tree with his fist . . . .

Agena repeatedly punched the tree with his fist, loosening the bark and ripping it off with his fingers. The bark came off in wide strips. Within two minutes, he had punched and ripped off an eight-foot strip, while Tengan had barely come down only one-third of the way.

Tengan threw down his chisel and admitted defeat. By now the village people had heard about the bet and had gathered around the tree, wondering how Agena had accomplished his feat. Tengan went off to the market place and bought the meat. With the help of the village headmaster and his family, both friends finished off the meat and a few extra jugs of sake.

*   *   *   *

If Agena was a great martial artist, it is only through the stories told about him that he can be truly appreciated.[3] One such story is of interest.

Agena frequently made trips from Gushikawa to Shuri to take lessons from Matsumura.[4] One day, after a hard workout with his teacher, Agena and his friend, Tengan Matsu, decided to take an alternate route back to his village. While passing Katabaru village, they heard a loud pounding.

Curious, they went to the source of the noise and found themselves in front of a cooperage, where wooden casks and tubs were made. Tengan, in one of his cocky moods, let all within hearing distance know in no uncertain terms that Gushikawa village produced the best of everything.

"Around here," Tengan raised his voice, "people use the *kama* (sickle) to cut bamboo. We in Gushikawa never use the kama."

The Katabaru cooper, sitting in front of his shop cutting bamboo strips with a kama to make a barrel, stopped what he was doing and looked up.

Tengan continued, "In Gushikawa we use our hands. The kama should be used for fine precision work to shave off the rough edges. That is all."

By now the cooper was becoming irritated. He had watched as Tengan strutted around and could no longer check himself. "You there!" the cooper blurted out, "If you can perform as you claim, I will give you fifty yen. But if you cannot, what will you give me?"

"We have no money," Tengan announced, "but I'll tell you what. If we fail, we will leave our clothes."

"Well, your clothes are not worth fifty yen, but they will do."

"You see this fellow here?" Tengan pointed to Agena. "He is the weakest and least skillful of the men in Gushikawa village, I will let him do do it, if you don't mind."

The cooper shrugged his shoulders. "The boy? Why he's nothing more than a stripling." But he nodded his head in agreement and went into his shop.

Tengan whispered to Agena, "The cooper thinks he is getting off with a cinch. Just this once, and I promise never to pull a prank such as this again."

The cooper emerged from his shop with a bamboo pole three inches in diameter. Agena grabbed the

While passing through Katabaru village, they heard a loud pounding.

86

bamboo and crushed it with his hand, asking, "How many pieces do you want?" He then tore off strips with his fingers as the cooper stared in disbelief at the fantastic display of strength.

"I wonder what the full-grown men in Gushikawa can do?" the cooper muttered, and he handed Tengan fifty yen.

* * * *

During Agena's time, there was one large public bathhouse[5] in Gushikawa village. This bathhouse still stands in testimony to the fantastic skill exhibited by Agena one fine winter afternoon.

Agena made it a ritual to soak himself in the bath every afternoon. The bathhouse assistant, Tengan Yama,[6] a distant cousin of Tengan Matsu, longed to see Agena's secret techniques. He pestered Agena daily, to reveal some of his secret techniques, but to no avail.

One fine winter afternoon, as Agena was soaking himself in the bath, Tengan Yama approached him and said, "I have never had the pleasure of seeing any secret techniques of a karate master. Please show me. I am an old man, and before I die, I want to have the pleasure of seeing your technique at least once."

As Agena was in a good mood, he smiled, stood up and said, "Take a good look, Yama!" He stabbed at the partition separating the men and women's sections with both hands and sat down.

Yama waited for a moment, rubbed his eyes and said, "I don't see any secret. What is the secret?"

"Look at the partition. There is my secret, if you want to call it a secret," Agena said then continued soaking himself.

Yama looked at the partition, then his eyes opened wide in amazement for there were ten holes where Agena's fingers had penetrated it. Agena had stabbed with such blinding speed that the old man thought he had merely made a motion in the air.

Tengan Yama could not keep his mouth shut. He told everyone he saw about the incident, and when people disbelieved him, he took them to the

. . . . there were ten holes where Agena's fingers had penetrated it.

bathhouse and showed them the holes. The story soon spread over Okinawa.

People came from far and near, the believers and skeptics alike. They all came to see Agena's feat. Tengan Yama, being a shrewd individual, raised the price of the bath fee. As more and more people came to see the bathhouse, Yama became wealthy, and the bathhouse became a sight-seeing attraction. Finally, the martial artists came, and Agena's fame grew proportionately to the number who went home and spread the word.

One particular sensei named Itokaze brought along all his students to see Agena's feat. Itokaze said, "Only a meijin could have done it."[7]

* * * *

... the village headmaster sounded the alarm, and all gathered in the square.

In 1920, at age 50, Agena probably performed his greatest feat. This was a time of severe drought, and water was carefully stored in barrels. One day, the village headmaster sounded the general alarm, and all gathered in the square. The headmaster spoke to everyone, "I have received word that many of the water barrels are leaking and, before we can get a cooper to come to this tiny village, we will have lost most of our water. This is a terrible crisis. Has anyone a suggestion?"

"Call Agena! He lives here in this village. We don't need a cooper. He can help us," someone yelled out from the crowd.

Agena, upon call, repaired the barrels with his bare hands. He tightened the hasps with only his fingers, to the amazement of all those in view.

There are many episodes about Agena and his steel fingers, but it is said he never hurt another human being, and in times of self-defense, merely subdued his assailants rather than killing them.

He died in 1924 at the age of 54.

NOTES FOR AGENA TAIRAGWAA

1.Feudal Japan had a rigidly hierarchical system called shi-no-ko-sho (warriors-farmers-artisans-merchants). It was practically impossible for any of the lower classes to become a samurai. In some rare cases, it was possible through adoption by a noble.
2.You will never see Agena in a dojo keizu (geneology), since he

never propogated a school. Like Miyamoto Mushashi with his sword, Agena could not transfer his ability into an educational system.

3.Some of the legends border on the supernatural, especially those concerning his jumping ability, which I have elected to leave out.

4.As a youth, he took lessons from Matsumura, who was over 80 years old at the time. It is said that Matsumura instilled a love and respect for the kata in Agena, something few people realized.

5.In villages which compared in size with Gushinkawa, it was almost impossible to find a private home with a bath (o-furo), particularly among the common people. Most people took their baths in a public bathhouse.

6.Tengan Yama was part-owner of the bathhouse and assistant to the village headmaster, his partner. Tengan collected the bath fees and also saw to it that the hot water boiler always worked properly.

7.Itokaze noted that the partition separating the two sexes was approximately three-quarters of an inch thick, and was nailed from the women's section.

Gichin Funakoshi

IF THERE IS ONE MAN WHO COULD BE
CREDITED with placing karate in the position it
enjoys on the Japanese mainland today, it is Gichin
Funakoshi. This meijin (master) was born in Shuri,
Okinawa, and didn't even begin his second life as
harbinger of official recognition for karate on the
mainland until he was fifty-three years old.

Funakoshi's story is very similar to that of many
greats in karate. He began as a weakling, sickly and in
poor health, whose parents brought him to Itosu for
his karate training. Between his doctor, Tokashiki,
who prescribed certain herbs that would strengthen
him, and Itosu's good instruction, Funakoshi soon
blossomed. He became a good student, and with
Asato, Arakaki and Matsumura as his other teachers,
great contributions were made to his developing
expertise and his highly disciplined mind.

When he finally came to Japan from Okinawa in
1922, he stayed among his own people at the
prefectural students' dormitory at Suidobata, Tokyo.
He lived in a small room alongside the entrance and
would clean the dormitory during the day when the
students were in their classes. At night, he would
teach them karate.

After a short time, he had earned sufficient means
to open his first school in Meishojuku. Following this,
his shotokan in Mejiro was opened and he finally had

a ' place from which he sent forth a variety of outstanding students, such as Takagi and Nakayama of Nippon Karate Kyokai, Yoshida of Takudai, Obata of Keio, Noguchi of Waseda, and Otsuka, the founder of Wado-Ryu karate. It is said that in his travels in and around Japan, while giving demonstrations and lectures, Funakoshi always had Otsuka accompany him.

The martial arts world in Japan, especially in the early Twenties and up to the early Forties, enjoyed an unprecedented boom. During this period, the ultra-nationalists were riding high, and they looked down their noses at any art that was not purely Japanese. They looked down on Okinawan karate and called it a pagan and savage art.

Funakoshi overcame this prejudice and finally gained formal recognition of karate as one of the Japanese martial arts by 1941.

Needless to say, many karate clubs flourished on mainland Japan. In 1926, karate was instituted in Tokyo University. Three years later, karate was formally organized on a club level by three students: Matsuda Katsuichi, Himotsu Kazumi, and Nakachi K. Funakoshi was their teacher. He also organized karate clubs in Keio University and in the Shichi-Tokudo, a barracks situated in a corner of the palace grounds.

Funakoshi visited the Shichi-Tokudo every other day to teach and was always accompanied by Otsuka, reputed to be one of the most brilliant of his students in Japan proper. Otsuka's favorite kata was the *Naihanchi*, which he performed before the royalty of Japan with another outstanding student named Oshima, who performed the Pinan kata.[1]

One day, when Otsuka was teaching at the Shichi-Tokudo, a student, Kogura, from Keio University who had a *san-dan* degree (3rd-degree black belt) in *kendo* (Japanese fencing) and also a black belt in karate, took a sword and faced Otsuka. All the other students watched to see what would happen. They felt that no one could face the *shinken* (open blade) held by a kendo expert.

All the other students watched to see what would happen.

Otsuka calmly watched Kogura and the moment he made a move with his sword, Otsuka swept him off his feet. As this was unrehearsed, it attested to the skill of Otsuka. It also bore out Funakoshi's philosophy that kata practice was more than sufficient in times of need.

* * * *

In 1927, three men, Miki, Bo and Hirayama decided that kata practice was not enough and tried to introduce jiyukumite (free-fighting). They devised protective clothing and used kendo masks in their matches in order to utilize full contact. Funakoshi heard about these bouts and, when he could not discourage such attempts at what he considered belittling to the art of karate, he stopped coming to the Shichi-Tokudo. Both Funakoshi and his top student, Otsuka, never showed their faces there again.

They devised protective clothing and used kendo masks in their matches .

* * * *

When Funakoshi came to mainland Japan, he brought 16 kata with him: 5 pinan, 3 naihanchi, kushanku dai, kushanku sho, seisan, patsai, wanshu, chinto, jutte, and jion. He kept his students on the pinan and naihanchi kata for at least three years before they progressed to the more advanced forms. The repetitious training that he instituted paid dividends; his students went on to produce the most precise, exact type of karate taught anywhere.

Jigoro Kano, the founder of modern judo, once invited Funakoshi and a friend, Makoto Gima, to perform at the Kodokan (then located at Tomisaka). Approximately a hundred people watched the performance. Gim, who had studied under Yabu Kentsu as a youth in Okinawa, performed the naihanchi shodan, and Funakoshi performed the koshokun (kushanku dai).

Kanso sensei watched the performance and asked Funakoshi about the techniques involved. He was greatly impressed. He invited Funakoshi and Gima to a *tendon* (fish and rice) dinner, during which he sang and made jokes to put Funakoshi at ease.

GICHIN FUNAKOSHI

Irrespective of his sincerity in teaching the art of true karate, Funakoshi was not without his detractors. His critics scorned his insistence on the kata and decried what they called "soft" karate that wasted too much time. Funakoshi insisted on *hito-kata sanen* (three years on one kata).

Funakoshi was a humble man. He preached and practiced an essential humility. He did not preach the humility of virtue, but a basic humility of a man who is rooted in the true perspective of things, full of life and awareness. He lived at peace with himself and with his fellow men.

Whenever the name of Gichin Funakoshi is mentioned, it brings to mind the parable of "A Man of Tao (Do) and a Little Man." As it is told, a student once asked, "What is the difference between a man of Tao and a little man?" The sensei replies, "It is simple. When the little man receives his first *dan* (degree or rank), he can hardly wait to run home and shout at the top of his voice to tell everyone that he made his first dan. Upon receiving his second dan, he will climb to the rooftops and shout to the people. Upon receiving his third dan, he will jump in his automobile and parade through town with horns blowing, telling one and all about his third dan."

The sensei continues, "When the man of Tao receives his first dan, he will bow his head in gratitude. Upon receiving his second dan, he will bow his head and his shoulders. Upon receiving his third dan, he will bow to the waist and quietly walk alongside the wall so that people will not see him or notice him."

Funakoshi was a man of Tao. He placed no emphasis on competitions, record breaking or championships. He placed emphasis on individual self-perfection. He believed in the common decency and respect that one human being owed to another. He was the master of masters.

Funakoshi died in 1957 at the age of eighty-eight, having humbly made a tremendous contribution to the art of karate.

His critics scorned his insistence on the kata and decried what they called "soft" karate . . .

THE WEAPONLESS WARRIORS

NOTES FOR GICHIN FUNAKOSHI

1.Funakoshi sincerely believed it would take a lifetime to master a handful of kata and that sixteen would be enough. He chose the kata which were best suited for physical stress and self-defense, stubbornly clinging to his belief that karate was an art rather than a sport. To him, kata was karate.

Kanryo Higashionna

HIGASHIONNA (HIGAONNA) WAS BORN IN NAHA, Okinawa, in 1845.[1] Even today, he is known and respected for having taught Miyagi Chojun, the father of modern *goju-ryu*. Few living karateka, however, have any knowledge of what a superlative martial artist Higaonna was in his own right.

Kanryo Higashionna flashed across the karate sky like a brilliant comet and, in his wake, left a legacy that is carried on today by all goju practitioners. In his time, there were two Higashionnas: West Higashionna and East Higashionna.[2] Both were prominent sensei, and the question of which was better often arose.

It was never officially settled but, if history is any judge, we have to observe that Kanryo (West Higashionna) left his mark, while his counterpart did not. In his case, the criteria is not what he personally achieved, but what he accomplished as a teacher.

The tale of Kanryo began when, as a youth, he went to work for a rich tea merchant. His employer made periodic trips to Fukien province, China, where he purchased tea. On one of the trips, the merchant was badly beaten by Chinese bandits. Kanryo, who adored the merchant, made up his mind to study the martial arts. For the first time, he understood the meaning of the motto, "The first principle of self-defense starts with oneself."

On one of his frequent trips to China, the merchant talked for a long time to his compradore.[3] Kanryo, who did not understand Chinese, watched and noted both men nodding their heads from time to time. Every once in awhile, the merchant would glance at Kanryo and smile. Finally, they stood up, and the merchant beckoned to Kanryo and said, "I am leaving you in the care of Mr. Woo Lu Chin, who is a gentleman. When I return to Okinawa, I shall apprise your parents of my decision. You shall be well taken care of here. You shall learn trade, management and the martial arts, since Mr. Chin is not only an excellent dealer, but also a master of the martial arts." With that, the merchant left.

In the beginning, Kanryo had difficulty learning the Chinese language and could not make any progress in his knowledge of trade or the martial arts. He gradually became quite proficient in the tongue and was asked to sit and watch Woo Lu Chin lead his martial arts class through its training sessions. He was amazed at the differences between what Chin taught and the karate practiced in Okinawa.[4] He looked forward to the martial arts class everyday with anticipation.

... the merchant said, "Kanryo, I'm taking you home."

One day, the Chinese master turned to Kanryo, saying, "Do you have this art in Ryukyu? If not, why don't you learn this art thoroughly?" Kanryo was overjoyed. He tackled the training with a vigor not exhibited by the other students. Soon, two years had passed since the merchant had left Kanryo in China.

Then one day, there was great activity in the compradore's house. Trading ships had come in from the Ryukyus (Ryukyu Islands, one of which is Okinawa), and the tea merchant was among them. He saw Kanryo looking fit and was pleased. He asked him what he had learned during his stay. While they were talking, the compradore entered and went off to one side to converse with the merchant. When they returned, the merchant said, "Kanryo, I'm taking you home."

The compradore protested, "Kanryo is now learning my art. If he returns to Okinawa now, it would be to my shame as he has not yet mastered the art. People would say that Mr. Woo Lu Chin is not a good teacher after all."

The merchant turned to Kanryo and asked, "What do you think? The decision is yours to make."

Chin took this opportunity to add, "Let him stay for another three to five years. I will polish him up to my satisfaction. Kanryo, it is up to you to decide."

"I shall remain," Kanryo replied without hesitation.

*   *   *   *

Thus the tea merchant returned to Okinawa without Kanryo. History becomes vague at this point. Some accounts say that Higashionna stayed for five more years, while others say that he stayed until the age of thirty-five. There is general agreement that Kanryo Higashionna stayed in China at least seven years and not more than eighteen.

Kanryo finally mastered the particular art, still unknown in the Ryukyus. One day in the middle of April, his teacher said to him, "I did not allow you to travel in China during your stay because I wanted you to learn and study. Now the time has come, so let us travel."

Together, they traveled over a wide region of central China. Kanryo was impressed by the vast size of the country, which was overwhelming to the youth who had been raised on the island of Okinawa. As they reached the end of their travels, they entered a valley that stretched out into the flatlands. There they encountered a huge person, who blocked their way and demanded payment for passage.

"What if we refuse to pay your demands? What will you do then?" asked his teacher.

The tall wayfarer smiled grimly and pointed to their clothes. "Give me money or I shall take your clothes. I give you only enough time to make up your mind."

"I have a suggestion," the teacher began, "if you

... they encountered a huge person, who blocked their way and demanded payment for passage.

can beat this young man in combat, we will gladly give you all our money and clothes."

The bandit laughed. "Why, this young man is no match for me, but if that is what you want, I agree."

The teacher turned to Kanryo and said, "This is your first fight, a good opportunity for you to test your skill and knowledge. As you are well aware, there is training only in forms in my system. Now the training is over."

Kanryo fought with the bandit for about 15 minutes before the bandit suddenly leapt into the air with a double kick. Kanryo hit the bandit's leg and knocked him down while clutching the man's cheek and wounding his face with a finger strike. The bandit yelled in pain and fled.

Kanryo's teacher approached him. "I have taught you all I know. When you return to Okinawa, never try to harm anyone. Use your art only for self-defense."

. . . the bandit suddenly leaped into the air with a double kick.

Kanryo finally went back to Okinawa and practiced what he had learned in China.

During his long absence, many spoke of Kanryo and the unknown art. Students flocked around him, eager to learn. He opened a dojo across from the *Okinawa Shimbun-Sha* in Tondo-Naha-shi, where passersby heard the noises of the martial artists practicing.

Gradually, a solid core of students emerged, among them were Miyagi and Kyoda. The *sanchin dachi* (a stance) was practiced incessantly, and the basics were repeated with pedantic regularity. Sometimes the young students would try, with permission, to choke the master by tying an obi around his neck and pulling on both sides in a tug of war. They might have better spent their time trying to choke an oak tree.

At other times, Kanryo good-naturedly invited students to punch his stomach with all their might. During festivals, he would stand on a veranda with a rope tied around his ankles. A man would try to pull him down while he was standing in the sanchin-dachi No one ever succeeded.

KANRYO HIGASHIONNA

NOTES ON KANRYO HIGASHIONNA

1.Kanryo Higashionna (1845-1915)—He passed away in the same year as his friend, Itosu Yasutsune. Although both taught different styles, they were very close friends and remained so to the end.

2.Kanryo, known as West Higashionna, was a solidly built, thick-set and huge by Okinawan standards, while East Higashionna was thin and wiry. Both were superlative martial artists and called "tan-me," a title denoting respect and affection.

3.Compradore: a Chinese agent engaged by a foreign establishment in China to have charge of its Chinese employees and to act as intermediary in business affairs.

4.Karate in Okinawa at that particular time was practiced as handed down by Sakugawa and Matsumura.

NAHA-TE

Miyagi Chojun

IN THE ISLAND OF KAUAI, in the Hawaiian achipelago, an Okinawan newspaper, *Yoen Jiho Sha*, printed the following article on May 1, 1934: "Long awaited Mr. Miyagi finally arrives . . . Chojun Miyagi, the recognized authority of Ryukyu karate and master of immeasurable skill, has prepared to visit Hawaii on invitation . . . Mr. Miyagi is the master at Taiiku Kyokai, operated by the government of Okinawa and, as far as his profound knowledge in his art is concerned, no one in all of Okinawa perfecture can equal him. Prior to his departure for Hawaii, he conducted a one week seminar sponsored by the Okinawa branch of the Dai Nippon Butoku-Kai."[1]

Miyagi Chojun, an extremely quiet man, was born to nobility in Naha, Okinawa. The name Miyagi is a Japanese derivation. The Okinawan name is Miyagusuku.

Miyagi started to learn karate at the age of nine, and by the age of 20, he became Higashionna's disciple. He later went to China as his teacher had done before him and studied Zen, as well as the martial arts, in a temple in Central China.

After many years, he returned to Okinawa, formulated the Goju-Ryu principles and founded his own school. He developed the *sanchin* and *tenso* forms, incorporating the *shorei* movements with Zen breathing as he had learned in China. He devoted his life to spreading his art and spent a fortune traveling in the Pacific area, going to Hawaii then to Kyushu and other parts of Japan.

After the defeat of Japan in the Pacific War, he went back to Okinawa from mainland Japan and settled in Ishikawa. The years immediately following the war were very lean for the families in this area, and the entire village would go out into the fields to harvest in cooperative effort. Miyagi was very quiet and no one knew who he was as he never spoke about himself or karate.

At harvest time, some men told Miyagi to make tea, which was a woman's job. They felt he could not take the hard labor in spite of his huge body; they mistook Miyagi's quietness for timidity. On several occasions during the lineup for rations, he would give his place to an old woman or man and start all over again at the end of the line. Sometimes young ruffians would jostle him and push ahead of him in the line, and he would only smile. His humility was so genuine that he silently made tea and washed dishes while the so-called robust men went into the fields and harvested the grain.

Miyagi was very quiet and no one knew who he was . . . .

After each day's harvest, several men would lift the huge loads of bale onto trucks for transportation back to town. On this particular day, the bales were larger than usual because the foremen were anxious to get back to town early. The loads were of extreme size, and the men were struggling to load them on the trucks. Seeing this, Miyagi told the men to step aside and lifted the loads himself, quickly and without strain.

His feat of strength amazed the men, and stories of his act circulated all over the island. Men came from all over Okinawa to see this strong man, and karate experts were astonished to see Miyagi Chojun in Okinawa for they believed that he was still in Japan. When the martial artists learned of his promixity in Ishikawa, they flocked to him for lessons.

Whenever exceptional feats of strength are told, the name of Miyagi Chojun comes to mind. Journalist Tojuda Anshu wrote the following revealing account:

"As a youth, in the year 1928, I became a student of the great karate master, Kyan Chotoku. I was then nine years of age and considered it a great honor to train at Kyan's dojo in Hishagawa.

"One day, to my surprise, I heard that my friend Yamakawa Iwasuke was taking karate from Miyagi Chojun. It was a day I shall always remember. Yamakawa took me to watch him train at Miyagi's dojo. It was the first time I saw Naha-te.[2] It was very different from Shuri-te. I watched the students practicing sanchin kata. It looked wild and savage to me.

"Then I saw Miyagi Chojun perform. I have not seen since, before, and now a man like him. I held my breath. Miyagi was simply amazing, just amazing. He exuded a vitality as fierce as a lion yet, you could see the innate gentleness and control of the man. If there ever was karate in perfection, I saw it then.

"Miyagi Chojun's training was scientific and severe. For certain periods of time, all the young boys would train at midnight, in the graveyard, to develop their minds. No one could advance to the next kata without first perfecting the (simpler) kata. It was basics, basics, and more basics with the kata thrown in-between.

"Miyagi Chojun awoke every morning at five o'clock sharp, practiced some kata several times, and hit the road. He would run about 10 kilometers, come back to the dojo, and do the kata again.

"In 1924, Taisho Ju-san-nen, Kano sensei and his leading disciple, Nagaoka,[3] came to Okinawa and gave a two-hour lecture and demonstration of judo. According to the *Asahi Shimbun*, it was a fantastic demonstration of human endurance and ability. Miyagi saw the demonstration

"He exuded a vitality as fierce as a lion . . . . "

accompanied by an old man named Matsu.

"After the demonstration, Matsu asked Miyagi if any karate expert could equal the endurance exhibited by Kano sensei and Nagaoka. Miyagi simply replied that any martial artist worthy of the name could perform for hours without drawing a heavy breath. The *Asahi Shimbun* heard about heard about it and asked Miyagi to perform and uphold karate. He finally agreed, after much pleading, and as the paper put it, 'Not for show, but for the sake of Okinawan karate.'

"Miyagi performed without pretension. Okinawa never saw anything like it. It was the performance of a karate meijin. Miyagi thrust his hand into a bunch of bamboos and pulled out one from the center. He stuck his hand into a slab of meat and tore off chunks. He put white chalk on the bottom of his feet, jumped up, and kicked the ceiling—leaving his his foot-prints on the ceiling for all to see. Spectators hit him with long bo (staffs) with no effect. He tore off the bark of a tree (with his fingers). And with his big toe he punctured a hole in a kerosene can . . . He did many more feats which had to be seen to be believed.

"He performed all afternoon, way past the two-hour mark. After the performance, Miyagi said, 'Any karate expert who trains properly can do all this. It is simply a matter of paying the price. Karate is a total commitment. I have not done anything that someone else cannot do, or, for that matter, you. There is no halfway measure. Either you do it or you don't. Nothing is impossible.' "

Miyagi Chojun was so pleasant in nature that there are not too many episodes of fighting or shiai in his life. He was extremely mild in temperament, and was the epitome of humility. He lived the art and never harmed anyone. He had promised his teacher that he

> "He put white chalk on the bottom of his feet, jumped up and kicked the ceiling . . . "

would never use karate to hurt another human being, and he kept that promise.

Once when walking home late at night, a stranger accosted him at a crossroad and challenged him to a match. Miyagi refused. The stranger insisted. Miyagi looked at the man and tried to talk him out of it. The stranger adamantly persisted. As he looked at the man, his teacher's words came back to him: "Never use karate to harm a human being. Only as the last means to protect your life."

So he decided to throw the person with *yoko-nage*,[4] a technique that his teacher had taught him. So he stood there and waited for the attack that he knew would come. When the man finally attacked, Miyagi avoided the blows and watched for a chance. He could see that the man was a skillful martial artist. Extremely careful, not wanting to hurt the man, Miyagi jumped from side to side, avoiding the kicks and punches the stranger threw.

Finally, in exasperation, the stranger gave a loud kiai and threw a wild punch. At that instant, Miyagi blocked the arm with a back-hand blow and threw the man into a clump of bushes alongside the road, then he left.

Miyagi Chojun died in Ishikawa, Okinawa, on October 8, 1953. He had the body of a bull and the spirit of a saint. He did not seek glory nor gain for he was a man of humility.

. . . . a stranger accosted him at a crossroad and challenged him to a match.

NOTES FOR MIYAGI CHOJUN

1.Haines, Bruce A., *Karate History and Traditions*, (Rutland, Vermont and Tokyo, Japan), 1968, pp. 123-125.

2.Although his teacher Kanryo Higashionna had introduced the Naha-te style, Chojun systematized it and named it Goju-Ryu (Go-Ju Ryu). Go, literally translated, means hard, and ju, literally translated, means soft. Therefore, goju-ryu translates as hard-soft style.

3.Nagaoka: one of the few 10th dans in judo history. He headed the judo section of Dai Nippon Butoku-Kai and taught at the Butokuden in Kyoto.

4.Yoko-nage: a throw similar to the judo yokoguruma, which was founded by Mifune at the Kodokan.

MORALITY IN KARATE

The most difficult task in teaching karate is to instill belief in the moral aspects of the art. Most students are interested in the immediate results of fighting techniques and care little about the morality which is the foundation behind them.

This raises the question, "If we are fully aware of the violence inherent in man's nature, are we not turning out killers? Are we not teaching an art that enables man to destroy man?"

The answer must be, as the great Okinawan masters have always answered, "Yes, we are fully aware of the violence inherent in man, and that the art of karate embraces within itself techniques to kill with the empty hand. But, there is a morality involved, woven in the fabric of karate, that controls the violence and the use of the art except under one condition—absolute necessity and dire peril."

The rhetoric is good, but the question itself is academic. How does one go about teaching fighting techniques and instilling morality at the same time? How does one accomplish the juxtaposition of fighting and morality at the same time?

The answer is found in the kata, the heart of karate. Kata is meant to train the mind, and is not intended solely for conceptual and intellectual self-defense. Indeed, to bring it in contact with the real self is its true purpose.

Kata, in the traditional sense, is a religious ritual. The art of karate does not mean the ability of technical excellence, which can be developed by physical training, but an ability of attaining a spiritual goal through the practice of the kata, so that the player plays against himself and succeeds in conquering himself.

THE WEAPONLESS WARRIORS

The basis of kata is in the concept *"Karate ni sente nashi,"* literally translated, "In karate, one does not make the first move." All kata begin with defense and end with defense. The kata instills the belief that the true karateka never strike first, and never strike in anger.

During the Satsuma occupation of Okinawa, a Japanese samurai, who had lent money to a fisherman, made a trip on collection day to Itoman Province where the fisherman lived. Unable to pay, the poor fisherman fled and tried to hide from the samurai, who was famous for his short temper. The samurai went to the fisherman's home and, not locating him there, made a search of the town. As his search for the fisherman proved fruitless, the samurai grew furious. Finally, at twilight, he came across the fisherman cowering under an overhanging cliff. In anger, he drew his sword. "What do you have to say?" he shouted.

The fisherman replied, "Before you kill me, I want to make a statement. Can you grant me this humble request?"

The samurai said, "You ingrate! I lent you money when you needed it and also gave you a year to pay, and this is how you repay me. Out with it, before I change my mind."

"I'm sorry," the fisherman said. "What I want to say is this. I have just started to learn the art of the empty hand and the first thing I learned was the precept: 'If your hand goes forth, withhold your temper; if your temper goes forth, withhold your hand.' "

The samurai was astounded to hear this from the lips of this simple fisherman. He put his sword back into its scabbard and said, "Well, you are right. But remember this, I shall be back one year from today, and you had better have the money ready." Thereupon, he left.

Night had fallen when the samurai returned home and, as was the custom, he was ready to announce his return when he noticed a shaft of light streaming from his bedroom through the door, which was slightly ajar.

He peered intently from where he stood and could see his wife sleeping and the faint outline of someone sleeping next to her. He was startled and exploded in anger as he realized it was a samurai.

He drew his sword and stealthily crept towards the room. He lifted his sword and was ready to charge into the room when the words of the fisherman came to him. "If your hand goes forth, withhold your temper. If your temper goes forth, withhold your hand."

He went back to the entrance and said in a loud voice, "I have returned." His wife got up, opened the door and came out with his mother to greet him. His mother had his clothes on. She had put on his samurai clothes to frighten away intruders in his absence.

The year passed quickly and, come collection day, the samurai made the long trip again. The fisherman was waiting for him. As the samurai approached his home, the fisherman ran out and said, "I had a good year. Here is what I owe you and interest besides. I don't know how to thank you."

The samurai put his hand on the fisherman's shoulder and said, "Keep the money. You do not owe me anything. I owe you."

* * * *

After World War Two, during the occupation of Japan, residents of a quiet street in Osaka were startled to hear the cries of men in anger and the anguish of a man in pain. It was early morning.

The people streamed out of their homes to find the source of the commotion. They stopped as they saw seven drunken foreigners beating up a native Japanese. The native was on the ground, bleeding.

"Please help me!" the beaten one yelled.

No one made a move. Japan had just lost the war, and the Osakans were afraid of retaliation from the occupation authorities if they interfered in an altercation involving foreigners. They watched helplessly as the drunks continued the beating.

Suddenly, someone pushed the drunks aside, lifted the badly beaten man, took him to the edge of the crowd and said, "Take this man to a hospital, quickly." Then he turned to face the drunks.

The drunks exploded in frustrated anger and attacked the lone samaritan. They punched and pushed the man around, venting their hostility and outrage on the man they considered a spoilsport. They tried their best to knock the man to the ground in order to kick him, but the man did not go down. He bled from his nose, and a small trickle of blood came out of his mouth. Otherwise, he was unhurt. He stood calmly and watched the seven men pound his body.

"Why doesn't he fight back? It is obvious he can take their blows. They may as well punch an oak tree for all the damage they are doing. They are like children milling around a grown man," the people muttered among themselves.

THE WEAPONLESS WARRIORS

One by one, the drunks realized that they were not making any headway against this man. They suddenly realized their fun was gone. The man was smiling as if to say, "Now little boys, don't you think the game is over? Go on home."

The seven stopped punching and slowly backed away from the man. They could not take their eyes off him. Fear set in. They looked at the crowd, suddenly panicked and fled.

The man, who was the recipient of the unprovoked beating by the seven, calmly wiped the trickle of blood from his nose and turned to the crowd. He bowed and calmly left.

In the crowd, a young man who had watched the whole scene, turned to the elderly man who was standing next to him and said, "Sensei, I recognize him. He is a karate sensei. He could have finished up the seven. I wonder why he let them beat on him like that?"

"You saw an example of the morality of karate. He knew the seven would have killed the poor man they were attacking, and he let them beat on him and vent their rage because he could take their blows."

* * * *

The achievement of self-perfection is more important to the martial artist who possesses it than his physical and technical ability.

Kata takes great faith, tenacity and hard work to master. Every time one practices the kata, his first move and his last move remind him of "karate ni sente nashi." It is stressed incessantly. "In karate, there is no advantage in the first attack."

The kata also has another advantage. In sports, there are physical adversaries. Without the adversary, a set of rules, judges and arbitrators, there is no contest.

The kata in itself is a teacher forever. One does not have to go to a dojo except to be under the eye of a sensei whose function is to see that one is going in the right direction.

However, many believe the kata is meaningless, probably because their first exposure to karate was in mere technique and the realm of physical fighting. Where the morality of karate is missing, there is no karate.

There once was such a man. Let us call him Kuwada.

Kuwada had begun martial arts training with the desire of becoming feared by all men. But he soon discovered there was no short-cut to his transformation into a master.

MORALITY IN KARATE

Discouraged by the incessant kata training, Kuwada asked his sensei, "When are we going to learn something else? I've been here for quite some time, and it's kata, kata, kata, every day."

When his sensei gave no reply, Kuwada went to the assistant to the master and made the same inquiry. He was told, "The kata training is to polish your mind. It is better to shave your mind than your head. Understand?"

Kuwada did not understand, and in protest, he left the dojo, embarking on a notorious career as the best street fighter in Shuri. He was tough. No doubt about it. "A fight a night" was Kuwada's motto, and he often bragged, "I'm not afraid of a living man."

One night, Kuwada eyed a stranger walking calmly alongside a stone wall. It irritated Kuwada to see such composure in a person. He ran to the cross section of the road and waited for the man to pass.

When he did, Kuwada jumped out and threw a punch, but the man avoided the blow and grabbed Kuwada's arm. As he pulled Kuwada toward him, the man calmly stared into his eyes. Kuwada tried to pull away, but he could not. For the first time in his life, Kuwada felt a strange emotion—fear of defeat.

When the man let him go, Kuwada ran, but he glanced back to see the man calmly walk away as if nothing had happened. Kuwada later discovered the man was a master of kata; a martial artist who had never engaged in a fight in his life.

He who conquers himself is the greatest warrior. This is the highest of platitudes for the karate master.

RANKING SYSTEM IN MODERN BUDO
Adopted by F.A.J.K.O., on March 27, 1971.

Ranks	Age	Title
Ju-Dan (10th) over 10 years after Ku-Dan	70 years or over	*HANSHI over 15 years after Kyoshi 55 years old or over
Ku-Dan (9th) 10 years after Hachi-Dan	60 years or over	
Hachi-Dan (8th) over 8 years after Shichi-Dan	50 years or over	*KYOSHI over 10 years after Renshi 40 years old or over
Shichi-Dan (7th) over 7 years after Roku-Dan	42 years or over	
Roku-Dan (6th) over 5 years after Go-Dan	35 years or over	*RENSHI over 2 years after 5th Dan 35 years old or over
Go-Dan (5th) over 3 years after Yo-Dan	under 35 years	
Yo-Dan (4th) over 3 years after San-Dan	under 35 years	
San-Dan (3rd) over two years after Ni-Dan	under 35 years	No formal title
Ni-Dan (2nd) over 1 year after Sho-Dan	under 35 years	No formal title
Sho-Dan (1st) at least three years	under 35 years	No formal title
Ikkyu (1st Brown) Nikyu (2nd Brown) Sankyu (3rd Brown) Yonkyu (4th class) Gokyu (5th class) Rokkyu (6th class)	No age specified	KYU (below brown identified by different colors) *However, all kyus are considered white relative to the black belt.

*TITLES: May not be given irrespective of how high the rank; awarded for exceptional
achievement and outstanding character.
*F.A.J.K.O.—Federation of All Japan Karate-Do Organizations.

BIBLIOGRAPHY

BOOKS: PRIMARY WRITTEN SOURCES

Funakoshi, Gichin, *Ryukyu Kempo Tode* (Tokyo, Japan: Bukyo-Sha, 1922)

Haines, Bruce A., *Karate's History and Traditions* (Rutland, Vermont & Tokyo, Japan: Charles E. Tuttle Co., 1968)

Ieshiro, Yukitake, *Karate Gokui Kyohan* (Tokyo, Japan: Yachiyo Shoin, 1955)

Kinjo, Hiroshi, *Karate no Narai Kata* (Tokyo, Japan: Yukishobo, 1970)

Konishi, Yasuhiro, *Zukai Karate Nyumon* (Tokyo, Japan: Kawazu Shoten, 1953); *Karate-Do Nyumon* (Tokyo, Japan: Airyudo, 1959)

Mabuni, Kenwa, *Goshin Jutsu Karate Kempo* (Tokyo, Japan: Karate Kenkyu-Sha Kobu-Kan, 1934)

Maeba, Nakahiro, *Karate no Narai Kata*, edited by Karate-Do Fukyu-no-Kai (Tokyo, Japan: Daido Shuppan Sha, 1956)

Miyagusuku, Hisateru, *Karate-Do*, edited by Funakoshi Gichin (Tokyo, Japan: Nichigetsu-Sha, 1953)

Nakasone, Genwa, *Karate-Do Daikan* (Tokyo, Japan: Kenkyu-Kai, Shutpan-Bu, 1954)

Oya, Reikichi, *Karate-no-Narai Kata* (Tokyo, Japan: Kinen-Sha, 1956)

Toyama, Kanken, *Karate-Do Daiho-Kan* (Tokyo, Japan: Kaku-shobo, 1960)

NEWSPAPERS

Butoku Shimbun: Tokyo, 1959

MAGAZINES

Black Belt: First issue to the present issue, Los Angeles, California

Karate Illustrated: First issue to the present issue, Los Angeles, California

Gekkan Karate-Do: May 1956—June 1957

GENERAL WRITTEN SOURCES

Bush, Lewis, *Japanalia* (New York: David McKay Co., 1959)

Draeger, Donn, and Smith, Robert W., *Asian Fighting Arts* (Tokyo, Japan: Kodansha International, 1969)

Embree, John F., *The Japanese Nation* (New York: Farrar & Rinehart, 1945)

Gluck, Jay, *Zen Combat* (New York: Ballantine Books, 1962)

Harrison, E.J., *The Fighting Spirit of Japan* (London: W. Foulsham & Co., 1913)

Herrigel, E., *Zen in the Art of Archery* (New York: Pantheon Books, 1953)

Kerr, George H., *Okinawa: A History of an Island People* (Tokyo, Japan, 1958)

Kaigo, Tokiomi, *Japanese Education: Its Past and Present* (Tokyo: Kokusai Bunka Shinkokai, 1968)

Moore, Charles, editor, *The Japanese Mind: Essentials of Japanese Philosophy and Culture* (Honolulu, Hawaii: University of Hawaii Press, 1967)

Nishiyama, Hidetaka, and Brown, Richard C., *Karate: The Art of Empty-Hand Fighting* (Tokyo, Japan: Charles E. Tuttle Co., 1960)

Nitobe, Inazo, *Japan* (London: Ernest Benn, 1931); *Bushido: The Soul of Japan* (Philadelphia, Penn.: The Leeds & Biddle Co., 1900)

Okuma, Shigenobu, editor, *Fifty Years of New Japan*, 2 vols. (London: Smith, Elder & Co., 1962)

Oyama, Masutatsu, *This Is Karate*, (Tokyo, Japan: Japan Publications Co., 1965)

Parker, E., *Secrets of Chinese Karate* (New Jersey: Prentice-Hall, 1963)

Robbins, Desmond, *"The Throw; The Blow; and The Know,"* *This Is Japan* (Tokyo, Japan, 1958)

Rudofsky, Bernard, *The Kimono Mind* (New York: Doubleday & Co., 1965)

Satow, Ernest M., *"Notes on Loochoo,"* Transactions of the Asiatic Society of Japan, vol. 1 (Yokohama, Japan: October 1872-October 1873)

Suzuki, Daisetz T., *Zen and Japanese Culture* (New York: Pantheon Books, 1960)

Wakukawa, Ernest K., *A History of the Japanese People in Hawaii* (Honolulu, Hawaii, 1938)

Webb, Herschel, *The Japanese Imperial Institution in the Tokugawa Period* (New York: Columbia University Press, 1968)